You Should Have Been There

by

Richard Digance

Other books by the author on Amazon;

Four Months Lost
My 100 Strangest Shows

Content within this book is the copyright of the author and it cannot be copied or reproduced without the express permission of the author.
For more details contact rdigance@btinternet.com

This book has been at a strange time in our lives, with the first ideas put down in September 2020. I therefore dedicate this book to friends and family who would hear these stories from the horse's mouth during better times.
Keep safe

About the author

Richard Digance is one of the vulnerable over-70s trying to survive the modern world and the problems it throws at us all. At such a testing time he returned to his first love of writing as the world of live theatre brought down its final curtain for a while.

After 11 years of television and 20 years of radio shows, he turned his back on the showbiz industry to return to his first love of writing and music. He was never one to live in the bright lights, choosing to settle in the quiet of the Wiltshire countryside. He built a recording studio where he composes reams of incidental music for film and television and he composed the music and songs for the audio book of Bill Bryson's best-selling book, The Road To Little Dribbling.

Richard was one of the great folk entertainers of the 70's along with Billy Connolly, Max Boyce and Mike Harding. His evergreen career has been acknowledged through numerous awards within both the music and entertainment industries, from a BAFTA Nomination as a television entertainer to a Gold Award from The British Academy of Composers and Songwriters in 2003. His first award was a Sony for the radio documentary Dying for a Drink.

He has supported, amongst many others, Steve Martin in the USA and Robin Williams at the London

Palladium and is one of a few folk-singers to be included in the Virgin Anthology of Songwriters for his important contribution to British comedy song-writing.

Richard was born in West Ham, London in 1949, the third child of Doris Digance, a sweet-factory worker, and Len Digance, a lorry driver for Ford Motor Company in Dagenham, Essex. His earliest ambition was to be a professional footballer, but after an injury that put paid to that idea, music and writing became his life after a somewhat late start.

He attended college in Glasgow and that's where and when the green light came on. His first media attention came with the BBC, where he originally worked with satirist Bernard Braden and proudly even wrote for Basil Brush.

He joined Capital Radio, London in 1978 and presented Britain's first ever folk programme on commercial radio.

His book, The Animal Alphabet, has been featured in 14 countries as a teaching aid for the English language including;

Fearon Teacher Aids Series, Grades 4-6, Illinois, USA
Canadian Ministry of Education-The British Columbia Foundation Skills Assessment, Vancouver Canada
Oxford University Press Anthology of Verse, book 5
The New Comprehensive Strategies 1-5, Book 3, The West Indies
People For The Ethical Treatment of Animals (PETA) Foundation, London
The Animal Alphabet, BBC series

Western Australia Learning Aids
New Language For Learners, Form 1, Swaziland
April 2015- The English Genie Course, book 6, India

Whilst others came and went Richard continued to perform his unique shows of songs, rhymes and stories in a way that has been admired by the industry and the public alike. His one-man shows have taken him around the world, and his writing skills have resulted in numerous books, plays and film-scripts.

During these uncertain times Richard has concentrated purely on his writing as opposed to performance, creating a discipline of daily sessions at the computer.

Contents

The Introduction
Chapter One – Hello
Chapter Two- Bob Dylan
Chapter Three – The Mohne Dam
Chapter Four – The Bread Delivery
Chapter Five – The Monument
Chapter Six – Gerald Ford
Chapter Seven – Joni Mitchell
Chapter Eight – The Battle of New Orleans
Chapter Nine – World Cup Winner
Chapter Ten – My Recording Studio
Chapter Eleven – Knebworth Festival
Chapter Twelve – The Blues Brothers
Chapter Thirteen – Florence Nightingale
Chapter Fourteen – Brian May
Chapter Fifteen – The Red Arrows
Chapter Sixteen – Playing Cricket At Lords
Chapter Seventeen – Walking In Memphis
Chapter Eighteen – Nelson Mandela
Chapter Nineteen – Pinewood Studios
Chapter Twenty – Ottery St Mary
Chapter Twenty-One – The Grand National
Chapter Twenty-Two – Robin Williams
Chapter Twenty-Three – Theatre Royal, Lincoln
Chapter Twenty-Four – Theatre Royal, Windsor
Chapter Twenty-Five- Bottom Line, New York
Chapter Twenty-Six – City Varieties

Chapter Twenty-Seven – Worthing
Chapter Twenty-Eight – Film Extras
Chapter Twenty-Nine – Whitechapel Road
Chapter Thirty - Mickey
The Little Things In Life
Acknowledgements

Introduction

Oh, you should have been there. Or, you would have loved it if you had seen it for yourself. I'm about to make those statements turn to reality with a little help of some vivid imagination. I'm returning to various interesting days of my life and I'm inviting you to come along with me and be by my side as they happen. They're all great moments that I enjoyed completely on my own, but they would have been much better if I could have shared them with someone else. That person is now you, so jump on board and come along with me.

Loneliness is a symptom often associated with creative souls such as myself, it's just that few other people notice as it's something creative bods don't really like to talk about. It just kind of goes with the job I suppose. Finding sanctuary is the first step towards being creative, be it learning to play a musical instrument, writing or anything else requiring imagination and subsequent seclusion to make it all happen.

Many of the great painters were described as loners, hermits, anti-social, unsociable objects who were a bit on the weird side, and for some that may well have been a fair appraisal, but not all of them. Actually, on second thoughts I would imagine most were just like that.

Think about it though, songwriting is a solitary passing of the hours, as is learning lines for an actor or actress, painting a picture, spending hours in a recording studio, or writing a book. None of these things are helped by having other people around, sticking their noses in and telling you how to do it. One thing's for sure, there's always someone around who knows how to do it better than you isn't there?

It's all a very solitary existence that can easily lead to loneliness and it happens over and over again. Just imagine that feeling of a sort of darkness and yet it ends for many with walking on stage or being centre-stage at an exhibition or a book-signing. It can all lead to a temporary feeling of despair, but loneliness is not the same as depression. The correct definition of the word is the quality of being unfrequented and remote, in isolation. I have often felt lonely in my work but seldom depressed. Yes, I've had my moments, particularly in recent times, but I soon manage to shake it off and get on with my life.

That quote, the definition if you like, sums up the feelings of so many during the year of 2020. For many it was the worst year of our lives and we all were responsible to our ourselves to find a way through the mental and financial messes we found ourselves in. Make no mistake, nobody was exempt, but those in the creative world, who have probably spent more time on their own than most, were quite possibly in a far better position to tackle the problem of isolation with a kind of inner knowledge and sanctuary, a feeling that they'd been there before whilst writing songs, books, poetry or painting pictures.

I admit, right now, to feelings of loneliness as I worked in self-inflicted solitude. The realisation struck me in 2020 when I read a book by someone I have admired greatly, along with the wicked enemy that attacked the world with a vengeance. Putting the two things together I felt it the right time to return to many of the situations I experienced when on my own, but with the intention of going back with you, dear reader, by my side. I have enjoyed so many wonderful times whilst on my own and I wondered what you would make of them. Would you find them as awe-inspiring as me? As I write this I don't have the foggiest idea what your reaction will be, but you are more than welcome to join me as I return to some wonderful days in my life.

It's quite difficult to explain but I'm trying hard. I'm in a solitary situation, but you are with me, enjoying the moment, so I'm not in a solitary situation at all. Does that make sense? I suppose, in a nutshell, I'm saying I would loved to have shared so many moments with someone else when no-one else was around. My god, that sounds so double Dutch to me but I think I know what I'm trying to say. It is down to you to come with me and see if you would have enjoyed the events as much as I did and then, just maybe, the enjoyment would have multiplied. We can but give it a try.

2020 has given more months on my own than I could have wished for, what with self-isolation, enforced solitary confinement and all the other rules and regulations that have seemed to change daily. I've stared at more walls than I thought I had in my house. I've thought about times gone by more than most historians and each time something comes into my head, something I enjoyed on my own, the idea keeps coming back to me that it would have been far more enjoyable if I'd had someone beside me to enjoy such experiences. Are you still with me, dear reader? Then let's get going as I have a good many years to troll through to recall my solitary escapades.

Chapter One - Hello

My life, so far I should add, has been well-lived, that's for sure. It took an awful lot of years to cram all the things I wanted to see and do into my lifetime, but I've reached a point in my life, with so many years behind me now, where I'm more or less happy I've done most things I set out to do and lots more besides. Frank Sinatra may have sung about having regrets but I'm very proud to say I have had but a few, if any.

It was during the lockdown of 2020 that I realised I enjoyed my own company so much, either writing, painting, or working away in my recording studio. Yes, the months passed by and we all certainly needed a bit of a break from the constant bad news, but on the up-side it gave me a chance to really decide if I was happy getting on with my life without an audience. The answer was a simple one, yes. I spent more and more time in my recording studio working on material as a source of enjoyment as opposed to commercial gains. I never expected to make money from my music anyway so it kind of took me back to my early days of self-isolation. I just played my guitar for hours on end never thinking of a financial return, a bit of a luxury until it becomes your living. I painted more pictures, particularly on old guitars I'd bought from charity shops and car-boot sales, and I wrote a couple of books too during the enforced exile. In my own way I was happy with such a weird existence.

I've lived many years in a goldfish bowl as an entertainer, often going aimlessly round and round like those poor things, exposed to both praise and scorn in fairly equal proportions it's fair to say, but that never really bothered me at all as it goes with the goldfish bowl territory.

Sitting around for months has given me a chance to reflect upon the great things I have done, but with a difference. Why? Because I came to the realisation I have done so many things when travelling around and being in places on my own as I went about my odd occupation, things I was never able to share with anyone, and so I thought the time had come to re-live with you some of those memories and share them with you in the process. How did this idea come about?

My good mate, Steve Hewlett, a top-rate ventriloquist, kindly sent me a book during lockdown 2020, the autobiography of movie star and musician, Steve Martin, someone I had the pleasure to work with in The United States many years ago. I learnt so much stagecraft from Steve Martin, as well as finding him a very personable but shy man, despite his fame. As I made my way through the pages of his life I couldn't help but notice so many similarities between his life on the road and mine. If someone as mega as Steve Martin could tell it how it was then I felt I could do the same, and this is the result. Steve Martin, in his book, admits to times of hopelessness and loneliness and trying to handle his strange occupation when he found fame and fortune. Although I never reached the dizzy fame heights as him I understood every single word he wrote in that book. I suppose we have all read and enjoyed many autobiographies in our time, I know I have, but this was the only one that captivated me fully with a firm belief that it could have been written by me, obviously with the different levels of fame and fortune. Steve Martin is a comedy genius and I remain proud to have worked with him.

Although he was brought up in Waco, Texas and me in East Ham, in the East End of London, the similarities were there, as you shall see.

The year of 2020 is one that none of us will look back on with the greatest of fond memories, that's for sure, as we all tried to combat the mental confusion and loneliness of it all. It was the most horrible time for those of us not old enough to have witnessed the horrors of World War Two. Blimey, imagine that, living through a World War. I'm sure our rotten year could never have been as bad as living through a World War for over five years, not knowing when the next bomb would fall from the sky, thoughts and worries that our grandparents endured for too long. My dad would have just shrugged his shoulders and told all around him to just get on with it and be thankful we hadn't had to endure what he endured. That is the connection between Waco, Texas and East Ham, our fathers, neither being that keen on Steve Martin or myself going into this strange and vulnerable industry. I wish I'd spoken to my dad more when he was alive but it was difficult to find common ground most of the time.

To make my dreams come true when a teenager I had to leave my parent's council flat behind and make my way into the unknown world of entertainment, just like Steve did, not knowing at the time what a lonely trail it would be at times. I'd moved away, in both senses, from my friends who were into The Beatles and The Rolling Stones, as I became inspired by the music of Bob Dylan and folk singer Woody Guthrie. I'd fallen in love with my brand-new guitar, which in turn, meant I'd fallen out of love with most of the things that were once a huge part of my life. After endless trips to my local youth club, enjoying the music of our resident bands The Small Faces and The Undertones, I'd settled into staying in every night trying to master my guitar. I'd gone with friends to see The Who at Hammersmith Palais, saw Roy Orbison at East Ham Granada and The Beatles at the very same venue, but it was all to change. It had to because I'd replaced my button-down Ben Sherman shirt with a duffle coat and a pair of Levis and my friends at the time made no sense of it at all. I had become weird in their eyes and I couldn't disagree. My education was minimal and yet I was growing into a young man of words. I started reading books as opposed to comics and I listened to words of songs more than melodies. It was all part of becoming a folk-singer I suppose.

During the day I worked in a shoe-shop in East Ham High Street and by night I was alone, apart from my new distanced friendship with Bob Dylan who I would never meet. Never meet your heroes they say, well there's no chance I'll ever meet Mr Dylan so there's no problem with that warning.

Many's the time I became lost in my new world and, some nights, I even forgot to go to bed. It was the life I had chosen and I soon realised I didn't need a multitude of friends to try to make headway. Quite the opposite really, I didn't need friends to make me smile. My dreams and aspirations made me smile instead. It sounds selfish but it wasn't meant to be. I was just happy in my own little bubble as I tried to be somebody and find myself. I had to get away, just like Steve Martin realised, and I did exactly that.

That's how I continued my early life in entertainment, having tons of friends on the outside yet very few in my private world. It was a situation that I think helped me through the daily grind of 2020 as I spent five months in self- isolation, never going further than my front gate because I was in the age group of the vulnerable, the possible victims of a wicked enemy. Then, as 2020 drew to a welcoming close, it was again the crowds of mainly youngsters, just like those Beatles and Rolling Stones followers, who got in the way of where I wanted to be as they partied and shouted in the distance and helped to close all the venues where I plied my trade. It reminded me, in a strange way, of the self-solitude I entered into to become a professional musician. Maybe those early years had helped me get through such a torrid time as 2020, I've no idea, but the similarities were definitely there. I knew I wasn't alone with such feelings anymore.

During the months of 2020 I thought back on so manly brilliant events and places I had experienced entirely on my own through the fifty years of being on the road. Many of the many memories that came flooding back made me smile and it was that very emotion that made me think I wanted to share with others, people like yourself. Obviously I wasn't always alone, I'm not a hermit by any means, but I thought it would be so great to re-visit places in my head, places where I'd been without company the first time around. And so this book began to take shape.

The bullet points rattled out like a machine gun and the time had come to think of all the times I wish someone had been by my side to enjoy what I was enjoying, times when there was no road crew or tour manager, no support act or driver, just me having a look at things around the world with no-one by my side. Needless to say, I enjoyed every minute and I'm going to enjoy them now all over again, but with you by my side. Let's go.

So, you're coming backstage with me, visiting places you never thought you'd ever see in your life, waiting at boring airports with me, bumping into people you never thought you would bump into, standing beside me at my easel as I paint, finding yourself in precarious situations that will definitely make you smile with either fear or trepidation. It's all a different slant to life on the road so forget stage performances and TV shows, I've written about those before and bored many people with such stories. This is the time to come along with me and experience the unseen part of my life when I did and saw so many things on my own.

Solitude may well be possible when experiencing with someone else after. Sanctuary may well be far more blissful when not having to taste it on your own. I've been around the block a few times and added more years to my life than I ever thought I would and now the time has come to go around another block but with a different mindset.

I've travelled many a mile
From Cornwall up to Carlisle
I've seen all England can show me
But still very few know me
Sometimes I want to get home
Spend a few hours on my own
With you, yes with you
You're the best friend that I ever knew

It's a long winding road I chose
Where it leads me god only knows
This is my own King's shilling
As each dream I had I'm fulfilling
Sometimes when my eyes are sore
I wonder what's it all for
So do you, yes so do you.
But it's dreams that help me get through

I still hear my father's voice

Who disagreed with my choice
A proper job he suggested
My long hair and guitar he detested
But now I leave it behind
His moaning is far from my mind
That's sad, oh so sad
That distant echo of dad

Chapter Two – Bob Dylan

To begin my lonesome travels I need to return to the 1960s and I bet you wish you'd been with me during those wonderful days of liberation, free love, a time when the whole world seemed to smell of something rather strange.

To become more familiar with the aspiring British folk scene I had to venture to the other side of London from where I lived. Yes, I was leaving Waco, Texas behind. There were a few bastions of folk music in the East End, but the other side of the city was far more vibrant, and therefore compelling. It meant taking a tube-train from East Ham station and travelling for over an hour to the west side of London. Walking to the station with my long hair and duffle coat made me feel like a trespasser in my home area, yet when I got off the train at the other end I felt a sense of belonging, a sense of freedom and self-expression. It was like walking into The Woodstock festival in my head.

One such journey took me to a small coffee house in Old Brompton Road called The Troubadour. I was a young, rebel teenager eager to find myself and I'd find the very place that would help me.

I'm about to take you in there too, by my side, so we start by giving you the visual image of a small coffee house, a very small coffee house with lots of vintage coffee pots hanging from the ceiling like Christmas decorations. We enter in and walk diagonally across to a small flight of stairs in the right-hand corner that led down to the cellar. Before I take you down the steep stairs that turn back on themselves, let me tell you about this iconic place.

The rebellious periodical Private Eye was first produced and sold there as a kind of underground magazine. It's also where the Ban The Bomb movement was founded before it expanded into the CND, the Campaign For Nuclear Disarmament. It has a CV as long as your arm, this tiny coffee shop that you could walk past without even knowing it was there. So, we have walked through small tables of bohemian types, sitting at tables, plotting and planning, possibly the things I've mentioned, or possibly not. We don't hang around on the ground floor though as the action we are seeking is down that rickety staircase, in the cellar below. They may all be in deep discussion about various important and rebellious issues but that's not why we're here, so it matters not. Two old boys are sat playing chess whilst smoking roll-ups, oh how times changed. They are harmless enough and certainly not politically incorrect as they would be in these modern times.

The cellar is small and musty with a capacity of no more than fifty or sixty sardines or forty or fifty people. To our right is a small area that serves coffee and we turn to our left and see a tiny stage protruding from a couple of alcoves where they probably stored wine, years before, as they were directly below a trap-door in the pavement above. One such alcove is no bigger than four feet by five feet, probably the smallest dressing-room in the whole world, and sitting in there, waiting to go on stage, is one certain Bob Dylan. Yes, the one and only Bob Dylan no less. My inspiration. There was no pa system necessary because the place was far too small and yet, even so, the tiny place smacked of great importance at the time and was well worth the train journey across London.

Just to digress for a moment, turning right as you leave The Troubadour, down to the traffic lights and turning left, you end up outside Earls Court where Dylan would play to thousands in later years. Although I never saw it myself, rumour has it that Led Zeppelin trotted off to the coffee house after doing a huge Earls Court gig so they could have a bluesy jam session to end their wonderful evening. That epitomises and confirms the reputation that The Troubadour had. I would loved to have watched Jimmy Page play his guitar so close to me.

Back to our own trip. Bob Dylan did his first ever London gig at The Troubadour. Martin Windsor and Redd Sullivan ran the folk club there and they both went on before the main act and, boy, did they have some lungs on them. Martin, who always wore a blue double-breasted suit, strange attire for a folkie, played a huge acoustic guitar with great gusto and Redd just stood beside him and sang very loudly, often with his finger in his ear or with his hands in his pockets. Martin looked like an old Richard Thompson and Redd looked like an old Art Garfunkel.

We take our seats about two rows back and Redd Sullivan introduces, all the way from America, Bob

Dylan. My heart pounds. Your heart pounds too. Can you believe this is really happening?

He didn't look up as he unscrewed himself out of the tiny dressing room and sat on the stage. There are various photos around that were taken during this gig, but they show him standing up. He was seated on a glorified milking stool. He wore a pale green tee-shirt underneath an unbuttoned dark denim shirt. I still remember how small Bob Dylan was, quite a diminutive chap and yet he was close enough to reach out and touch, not that he would have been that impressed as he was untouchable. He had very long fingernails in comparison to the size of the rest of his body and they were soon at work.

Without any kind of introduction, just a nod, he begins his set with Boots Of Spanish Leather and A Man Of Constant Sorrow, a set that ends with his rendition of Blowin' In The Wind, a song that became a huge worldwide hit for Peter, Paul and Mary. He didn't say much at all other than a rambling tribute to Woody Guthrie, enthralling stuff for me and the rest of the tiny audience. We'd all heard of Guthrie but none of us knew that much about him, other than that he sometimes sang with Ramblin' Jack Elliott who also appeared at The Troubadour.

The point I wish to make about that night at The Troubadour was that I went on my own, but can you imagine if you had been there? Wouldn't you have just loved sitting no more than three feet away from the mighty Bob Dylan as he sang out those magical words he strung together? I would loved to have shared that moment with someone, but I never did.

I visited The Troubadour many times in the few years that followed. I saw Sonja Kristina do a great solo gig there before she fronted Curved Air and there were others who played there who I sadly missed out on and amongst those performers I never saw were Paul Simon, Jimi Hendrix and Elvis Costello. Oh yes, I missed out on a few but at least we saw Bob Dylan didn't we?

I continued to make trips to Old Brompton Road as often as I could muster the train fare and I eventually got to know a few other folkies who frequented the place with certain regularity.

One in particular was Linda Peters, a beautiful singer who performed with Paul McNeill. Ironically they released a single of the Dylan song 'You Aint Going Nowhere' and, despite my shyness, I would chat with Linda as she was such a beautiful person and singer. She later married Richard Thompson and the rest, as they say, is history, or geography if you wish to change the subject. I saw Linda perform before I heard Sandy Denny for the first time.

Another ironic fact is that Sandy worked as a nurse in the very same Old Brompton Road, just down the road from The Troubadour. I never saw the great woman there, she who single-handedly created the electric folk/rock movement, but I did see her play at The Prince of Wales pub, at a club run by Rod Hamilton, also just down the road from The Troubadour, across the railway bridge and on the right. I wouldn't mind betting you would have liked to have been by my side at Rod's club too? Watching Sandy Denny perform was spine-chilling.

I performed at The Troubadour just the once, on a Wednesday night gathering fronted by guitarist Gordon Giltrap and it would be fair to say that I died on my backside. Yes, I went down like a French kiss at a family re-union and I'm more than pleased you weren't by my side to watch me shrink into a further, deeper oblivion without even trying on that particular occasion. I doubt if the 6 or 7 people in the audience remember it and I'm grateful for that.

The venue is still there, despite the financial crashes of 2020. It still has plenty to boast as both Adele and Ed Sheeran have apparently played there in more recent times. I hope that's true. It has a legacy that will live on forever.

As I mentioned, Bob Dylan went on to play at Earls Court to massive crowds and I so wanted to see him again but I couldn't get a ticket and so I took a train up to Newcastle City Hall, a birthday present from my mum, and I have to say I much preferred that night at The Troubadour where I have just taken you. That was special, although he didn't speak much on that night either.

It's almost time to take you somewhere else where I would have enjoyed your company and leave Bob Dylan to his decades of brilliant songwriting that would follow, but this just had to be the very first recall as he was such an inspiration to me. His Freewheelin' album especially changed the direction of my life completely and helped me carve my early beginnings as a musician, so the fact that you and I went to see him at that tiny venue in Old Brompton Road takes top billing as far as I'm concerned.

As a final thought, I was remembering just now how I ever came to hear about Bob Dylan in the first place, this mod of the 60s into the Beatles and The Rolling Stones. Well, my brother Leonard, who I haven't seen for over half a century due to him moving to Vancouver, Canada, was an art student at Goldsmiths College in London and he got into weird music through having weird friends. Hey, he was at art college after all. One day he brought a Dylan album home along with a jazz album by Andre Previn and J.J.Johnson and I started to play the albums when the rest of my family were out of the house. I became transfixed and my interest in folk music had begun. I wasn't that interested in the jazz stuff, never have been.

Chapter Three – The Mohne Dam

During the 1980s I did many shows to British troops posted overseas, from The Falkland Islands to the freezing cold, northern regions of Norway, from The baking hot Middle East to mosquito-infested Belize. However, the trip that stands out the most in my pursuit to make soldiers smile was a short tour of British bases in Germany.

I was part of a large crew of a few performers, TV directors and various technicians as we filmed a Christmas Special for ITV at The Berlin Wall. To stand there, where so many lost their lives in the search for freedom was a heart-wrenching experience, yet there was an additional experience which made me gulp even harder. I walked through Checkpoint Charlie, stared at Hitler's bunker where he popped his own clogs and stood in the hallowed rooms beside the Brandenburg Gate where President Kennedy made his famous speech, but they all fall short of where I'm taking you now.

Once again, it was something I did on my own, away from the other members of the crew, finding solace during a hectic filming schedule, and it was one of the most humbling occasions I have ever experienced. If you had been with me it would have affected you too, I'm sure of that.

It wasn't a desperate loneliness I suffered on this day in 1985 as it was a self-inflicted desire to be on my own for a while. It was a character-building moment, an excursion that made me realise the suffering of others during times of war. You should have been there.

I was born a few years after the end of The Second World War and so, thankfully, I never witnessed the pain and horror of such a time. I'd never really thought that much about it until 2020. There was I beefing on about the enforced lockdown and loneliness of not seeing my family and friends for six months when it suddenly struck me. What must it have been like during nearly six years of war? My Dad grumbled endlessly about how it had changed his life and I never really understood his protestations until 2020, the year that all our lives were changed and my performance career came to a grinding halt a few years earlier than I had planned.

We had a day off from the German shows and so I took myself off to see The Mohne Dam, scene of The Dambusters mission during World War Two, which was approximately 25 miles to the east of Dortmund. I would have loved to have that moment with someone and so I'm inviting you to come along too. So, with you by my side, we are about to stand at the foot of that dam and imagine what happened that historic night in 1943.

To understand the magnitude of this historic event it was an operation that hurt both teams involved in the Second World War, so let's not take sides here. 1.400 civilians died during the attack, washed away by the flow of water caused by the dam being breeched. Half of those who perished were Russian and Polish women who were slave labourers under the instructions of Adolf Hitler. 100 French prisoners working in an aluminium factory also perished, so it was an international, across the board loss. The aircrews involved in the Dambusters campaign were also multi-national with personnel from Australia, Canada and other countries.

To see the daunting, somewhat sinister structure rise into the sky was one thing, but to share that moment with someone would have made it more of a spectacle. I'm returning there right now and once again you are more than welcome to join me.

We stand, two little specks below the very part of the dam that was breeched by Guy Gibson and his various crews of 617 Squadron on 16th May 1943, on what was called Operation Chastise, with each Lancaster plane taking off from RAF Scampton in Lincolnshire, carrying Barnes Wallis's famous bouncing bombs.

So how high is this remarkable piece of history? Oddly enough it stands less than 60 feet above the water, only about as high as three double-decker buses, yet it seems much higher because of two gigantic towers on each end, a bit like the old Wembley Stadium. We look up and yes it seems much higher and to our right is a memorial that gives the reality of the fatalities. It is humbling;

'1,285 women, children and men dead in the flood. 181 citizens of the town, 721 foreign civilians and Prisoners of War.'

The tidal wave completely washed away numerous farms in their entirety as it cascaded down the valley and over 25,000 animals, pigs, cows and sheep, were washed away too. Of the 133 aircrew involved, 53 lost their lives. In truth, whatever side we are on, it was a human catastrophe, although regarded as a major success by bombastic Bomber Harris and the top brass of the RAF. We are left to judge for ourselves of course.

Away from the TV crew and the posh hotels, you and I stand together in the countryside on this day off and take it all in above a patch of obviously repaired wall where the bouncing bombs struck. There is a silence because history and the years thereafter have diluted the outcome, the massive destruction. The silence is deafening as we look around us. Yes, it happened right here in May, 1943 and yet it's so peaceful it is hard to imagine. I stand in total astonishment, we both do. I knew all about The Dambusters, I saw the film a few times too, and more relevantly my PA Tracey Hollis's great uncle, Fred Tees was one of those who survived. A gunner in the rear turret of the Lancaster plane C for Charlie, he was the only survivor when the plane came down due to gunfire in a field near Hamm.

I have lived this day in 1985 so many times since. I saw and felt it all with my own eyes and I really wish, thinking about it now, that I had shared such a thoughtful time with someone like yourself. But at least I haven't returned there on my own. I promise you it will remain deep in your thoughts. Yes, you really should have been there.

Those shows for British troops were an inspiration to me and they brought about various songs from just being there and feeling what our soldiers were feeling at the time. I'm sure you would have felt the same and possibly written a poem or two like this one, composed for a homesick soldier a few years my junior.

I see in your letter it's raining
You say the weather's been bad
But reading between the lines as I do
I see in your letter you are sad
But it's me that's a million miles from my home
Me that sits here alone
Tell them all down
The old Rose & Crown
I'm coming home

I'm coming home
Back home to you
Tell them all down
The old Rose & Crown
There will be some celebrating to do
I'm coming home
Back home to you
Tell them all down
The old Rose & Crown
I'll soon be in for a few

I can't speak too long
The money's all gone
It costs a fortune from here
But I just called to say
I missed you today
By the way I could strangle a beer
Baby must be talking by now
Give her a cuddle from me
I know I've travelled all over the world
But there's one place I'd rather be

I'm coming home
Back home to you
Tell them all down
The old Rose & Crown
There will be some celebrating to do
I'm coming home
Back home to you
Tell them all down
The old Rose & Crown
I'll soon be in for a few

The operator just came on the line
Said I have no more time
I won't say that I'll write
The chances are slight
It's good to hear you on the end of the line
There are so many things to say to you
So many things on my mind
As I lie back and think of old England

The places and faces that I left behind

I'm coming home
Back home to you
Tell them all down
The old Rose & Crown
There will be some celebrating to do
I'm coming home
Back home to you
Tell them all down
The old Rose & Crown
I'll soon be in for a few

Chapter Four – The Bread Delivery

My time as a radio presenter and producer at London's Capital Radio spanned from 1979 to 1983 and it was a highly enjoyable time of my life. And yet it was the epitome of loneliness at times, talking to a wall. It's time to rectify that and have you sitting beside me once again, just like you did at The Troubadour.

Having become a qualified radio producer at Elstree it enabled me to stretch my radio appearances way beyond the folk programme that I originally went to Capital Radio to present. Such programmes included Sunday Funday, the schools quiz R2D2 and the programme that you are about to sit beside me as I go on air, Midnight Special.

We are sat in Studio 4, a room the size of a kitchen in a one-bedroomed flat. In front of us is the desk that I 'drive' that's the term used, whilst I speak live on air to the people of London. I can reach out and touch all four walls, it's that small.

I was given a tip by the late Kenny Everett, who was also working at Capital at the time, and it was advice that proved invaluable. He told me to take a photograph of someone I knew into the studio and place it front of me on the console and talk to only them as I did the show. It worked. I wasn't talking to London at all, but to the person I knew in the photo. It calmed the nerves and made the show far more personal.

So, anyway, we're at the desk and I've pushed a chair up beside mine so you can be there. It's a bit of a squeeze but we manage it. There is now so little room I can barely move around to the turntable, the tape machine behind me from which I play various concert tracks, and the pile of cartridges by my right elbow that I need to load up every time there is a commercial break. The whole experience of Midnight Special is solitary confinement in the extreme. Fours hours, from midnight, obviously, to 4am, just sitting in a tiny cupboard of a studio playing music to Londoners.

The only link to the outside world was a telephone that listeners could call if they wanted a dedication. During the day such callers would have heard a telephonist on the other end who would pass messages to the disc-jockey live on air, but this wasn't during the day. I had no such telephonist, no such luxury, and so I answered the phone myself, something you will be doing shortly on my behalf, trust me. The phone never rings, it only flashes up a light on the receiver, and, believe me, the light will never stop flashing for the whole 4 hours, so you're in for a busy old time.

I presume when anyone thinks of a major radio station such as Capital Radio they think of a busy hive of media industry. Well, yes it was during the day, but at night-time it was a different kettle of fish. Although situated in the giant Euston Tower, a real skyscraper of a building beside the Euston Underpass, it gave the wrong impression because it was only on one floor and the rest of the building was taken up with offices related to MI5. When I presented Midnight Special for those three years I was the only person in the building other than an overnight security guard who spent the whole time chatting to his girlfriend on the phone downstairs. As I've already said it was solitary in the extreme.

One night in 1981, out of complete boredom, I had a bit of a lightbulb moment and it was this very night I'm returning to now as I take you into the dimly-lit Studio 4. Please let me set it up;

I realised during such hours of darkness that I was being listened to by mainly night-workers, burglars or insomniacs. Sometimes it was difficult to even stay awake and on two occasions I didn't even manage that, but those nights are of no consequence to this book in general and this night in particular. I invented a London Grand Prix for bread delivery drivers, so many of whom were carting their vans around London delivering bread and cakes for the high street shops and supermarkets in the middle of the night, doing their best to stay awake at the wheel at such an unearthly hour. The rules were simple.

'Hey guys, I'm all on my own here, just like you are, so if you're listening to my show while you're driving round town drop by and leave me a nice cake at reception. Be the first winner of My London Bakery Grand Prix. I'm waiting. Call me when you've dropped one off and I'll give you a name check.'

So, we sit here waiting for the action to start and you see the light on the phone begin to flash like part of the Blackpool illuminations.

The problem with being on the radio is you can't possibly have any idea who is listening, if anyone at all. Oh yes, they are listening alright.

You begin to take the phone calls for me, chatting to the listeners, and the first is a guy from Bartons Bakers in North London who tells you he's left a custard slice with the security guard downstairs. We declare him the winner and still the phone flashes like some kind of nutcase. You run down the stairs and grab the custard slice and we have half each, even though my slice should be bigger as I'm the presenter!

After about ten minutes or so there is a knock on the door of tiny Studio 4 and it's the security guard holding numerous cake boxes and bags in his arms. He looks bemused. London by night has gone totally bonkers in a small way. He obviously isn't listening to the radio whilst on duty so he has no idea what the hell is going on. I explain about the London Bakery Grand Prix and he shrugs his shoulders as if I have a screw loose. We take the cakes and I tell him that if any more turn up it's best that he leaves them in reception and I'll pick them up at the end of the show. We still fail to bring a smile to his weary face.

On air I'm consumed with reading out the names of the drivers and the bakers they are delivering to between the records. You scribble more names down and pass them to me and it's relentless. It's free advertising after all and it has really caught their imaginations. Ha-ha, you are now a Production Assistant at Capital Radio, the biggest commercial radio station in Britain, with your very own designated job of making a list of the calls and callers for me to mention on air. It's so much fun and great to have a kind of physical contact with people we will never know, with someone beside me for a change too.

By 4am the foyer looks like a patisserie according to Phillip Schofield who is taking over the reins when I come off air. As is always the case Phil brings me a cup of tea and realising you are with me he nips off to make you one too. It was the first time we had tea and cakes instead of just a cup of tea. The three of us laugh our heads off like naughty little children. All in one night you've become a production assistant and met Phillip Schofield who is all set to become one of the country's top television presenters.

The show ends and the administration takes place before I can leave the building and head for home. We list the music played on PRS forms, it wasn't done online back then, to ensure the musicians get their radio royalties before putting the records back in the racks for another week. We make our way down the sweeping staircase to where the security guard is sitting, surrounded by a sea of cakes and pastries, Phillip was absolutely right. I guess around 80 or 100 varieties in all and the foyer smells like bread and fresh cream. We say our goodbyes to the security guard and he grunts as usual, not even bothering to look up from his morning paper first edition. Don't take it personally, he's only ever grunted one or twice to me the whole I've been doing Midnight Special, let alone talk.

We both go our separate ways as dawn flickers in the sky as London wakes up, and I watch you head off with various cakes and a Capital Radio tee-shirt to remember the event. You look more than happy with your night in London with me and I'm so glad you enjoyed yourself. Maybe you ponder as you watch the cars in Euston Road and beyond. Do they have their radios on? Have they been listening to The London Bakery Grand Prix from that little cupboard where you were sitting? The answer is probably yes they were. You want to shout out at the top of your voice that it was you who took the calls from the delivery drivers but it's pointless, but you have gained an insight into the world of radio.

The lonely presenter, plus one, linking with the lonely van driver or the lonely person in their bedsit. Somehow it came together and the job was done. I think back now on how many lonely people rely on that personal interaction with the radio. Back to back music like so many modern radio stations play today as a modern format doesn't really provide that. There are still many lonely people around, times don't change that much. I wonder if you remember that night we brought London to life and had a good laugh.

As a footnote, I ran The Grand Prix for a couple of weeks before the novelty of it all ran dry. After a couple of weeks a few baker's vans used to be waiting outside the studios when I went on air to make sure they were winners of the race. They say little things please little minds but it was more than that because we joined together to ease the boredom of working through the night whilst others slept peacefully in their beds, totally oblivious of the fun that was going on in the hours of darkness. I reckon I put on quite a bit of weight during that time, what with all those cream cakes.

I remember on another occasion I announced I'd run out of cigarettes and I had an equally successful result, leaving the studio with a good few dozen packets of fags from passers-by. Yes, everyone smoked back then and smoking in the studio was allowed and the odd fag helped me stay awake through those long and lonely hours taking to that photograph that Kenny EDverett had suggested.

I left Capital Radio in 1984 but I took some amazing memories with me. I hope it was an amazing memory for you too.

I've often recalled that strange event to make up poems of other unlikely Grand Prixs. When performing at corporate events in the years that followed I would write a poem for the company, relaying a ridiculous story, just like you and I did on that night. They loved the personal references and it became a strong part of my corporate act. And it all began with you taking those calls and writing down the names of those who were leaving us edible goodies in the middle of the night, as equally bored and lonely as us. Here is such an example;

This is the tale of Fred Higgins
A man both brave and defiant
A man who once won the British Grand Prix
In a sooped-up Robin Reliant
To be honest he didn't even mean to take part
He had his wife and kids in the back
So imagine both Fred's and his family's surprise
When they ushered him on to the track
Unfortunately Fred drove to the wrong gate
To the driver's enclosure he steered
The bloke checking tickets had nipped for a fag
Fred waited, but no-one appeared
It wasn't until he got out onto the grid
They all realized someone had blundered
It was the only car there with a roof-rack
So out the mechanics all thundered

'We thought you weren't coming,' one of them said
Much to Fred Higgins' surprise
'So this the prototype engine eh?
What a brilliant, brilliant disguise
There was a dice on the mirror a nodding dog
In the back
And a green velvet steering-wheel cover
'At the moment top speed's about twenty five or thirty'
The mechanics stared at each other

Within seconds the car was back in the pits
Bolts were undone in a flash
In English Fred's engine was knackered
In French it was lacking panache

They kissed Fred Higgins on both of his cheeks
'Best of luck son, in you climb'
Fred didn't like being kissed on both cheeks
He was bending down at the time
A dozen laps gone, Fred was back in last place
He decided to call in the pits
He took on some petrol, oil and new tyres
Two sausages, egg and some chips
Car after car went out of the race
Some crashed some simply broke down
But Fred's trusty Robin Reliant
Just kept on toodling around

Over the line the Reliant went
To win its first ever Grand Prix
The crowd went completely bananas
They turned yellow and hung from a tree
'How did I reach such incredible speeds?'
Said Fred to his team of mechanics
'I thought the roof rack and bags in the bag
Would mess up the aerodynamics'
They all put it down to Fred's driving
It was that which won it they reckoned
Particularly on that very last lap
When for the first time he changed up to

Second

When they presented Fred with the cup and champagne
You should have heard the crow roar
Fred said 'I did this all on three wheels,
Just imagine if I had had four.'

Chapter Five – The Monument

The Great Fire of London began on 2nd September 1666 and it raged until the 6th. It was a hell of a fire by all accounts, destroying 13,200 houses and 87 churches including the original St Paul's Cathedral. The population of London at the time was 80,000, less than the capacity of Wembley Stadium, and 70,000 of those were rendered homeless after the blaze. Amazingly only 6 people lost their lives, even though most lost their homes.

It's appropriate to bring you this chapter after the Capital Radio experience because The Great Fire of London began in a baker's shop in Pudding Lane. I doubt if they made custard slices in those days but, hey, you never know.

Being born and brought up in London it's history became of great interest to me. At school I wasn't bothered in the slightest to be honest. A school trip to The Tower of London was like watching paint dry, queuing up to see the Crown Jewels, what was that all about? Having jewellery for the rich being rammed down my throat did nothing for me and I laughed at those Beefeater chaps in their silly hats and bright orange socks. Soldiers? I would have taken them on any day looking like that.

One of my passions, as I grew a little older, was to take myself off to various parts of the city of London and try to feel its history, all on my own. More than that, I loved to discover stories that few others had bothered to find out about. Of course, there are endless sights to see in such a big place as London, but I had my favourite, as it really sparked my imagination. I'm going to take you to The Monument in Pudding Lane. Yes, you're coming with me so I'm not alone this time.

These days The Monument is difficult to find as it is surrounded, let's say engulfed, by large modern buildings. Yet it never used to be like that. So what exactly is The Monument? Why am I taking you there? By all accounts it is the very spot where The Great Fire of London began and it's a beautiful work of art that has become lost in the crowd and I feel it's time to re-light its fire and try to restore it to its former levels of glory, strange glory of course, and importance.

It's actually situated on the junction of Monument and Fish Street Hill and it's exactly 61 metres from Pudding Lane, where the fire apparently began.

As we climb the stairs from Monument tube station on the District Line, we are greeted by tall clusters of offices, nameless and faceless offices that look cold and forbidding. When I first visited The Monument on my bike as a kid it stood high and proud, but sadly no longer. It's a shame because it was built with incredible flair and imagination. Well of course it was, it was designed by Sir Christopher Wren, the clever man of the time. Now this chap really did get through some pencils as he also designed St Paul's Cathedral, plus Hampton Court Palace, The Royal Naval College at Greenwich and The Royal Hospital in Chelsea.

So, you and I stand side by side on my return and stare at his, Christopher's, smallest and yet most incredible works of architecture. Just look up, Sir Christopher Wren designed this. He once stood where we are standing right now and said 'That'll do.' Oh such a brilliant and creative man. He had help from a man by the name of Robert Hooke as you shall hear, but right now it's time to climb the 311 spiral steps that take us to the top. We are now 200 plus feet above London. Above our heads is a golden urn with flames protruding to remind us why we are here. Take a look down and imagine Pudding Lane as it used to be. The wooden shops all huddled together.

Smoke begins to bellow from the baker's shop beneath us and before you know it London is on fire. We all know about the fire but to stand above the very spot where it all began will really stir your imagination for sure. You are taken in even more when I tell you they built a small laboratory at the base of The Monument, and that was Robert Hooke showing his worth. The Monument was not just built as a statue of remembrance, but it was also London's first telescope, a little-known fact. Just imagine the eyes that looked up to where we are standing now to view the stars and planets overhead, trying to work out all the facts that were discovered years later. It was such an important symbol of both the past and the future and yet so very few people are bothered about it these days, such a shame. We have just brought it to life and both Wren and Hooke would both be so proud if they were also standing with us.

I have always been totally obsessed with this tiny monument, tiny by by modern-day standards at least, and now you see why. It even inspired me to write one of my silly poems, using the kind of imagination not befitting a grown-up;

In 1666 as all academics will know
The houses and shops of London caught fire
And being wood then
They didn't half go
Because they didn't have fire engines in them days
Nor fire blankets, nor fire hoses
In them days they didn't have nothing at all
Just rickets and tuberculosis

It started in a baker's in Pudding Lane
On a Thursday, at a quarter past one
When a baker called Thomas Farriner
Was slapping some ice on a bun
When a spark flew out of the oven
And set fire to a wooden hotel
And the first that anyone noticed
Was a horrible charcoaly smell
 Some thought the oven was faulty
And Tom had gone over to thump it
But that was a lie
He was keeping his eye
On, not buns in the oven but crumpet.

He was only a lad of tender years
He didn't care much for great fires or loaves
The ladies of London, interested Tom
And they passed by the baker's in droves
 Most were hospital nurses
Who had come to London and roughed it
It bit late I fear
Because the previous year
They'd had the plague
And millions had snuffed it

The fire got out of hand
As it roared down the Strand
Bond Street was one ball of flame
Yes Thomas Farriner's Monopoly board
Was ablaze from Pall Mall to Park Lane
Now historians of course had distorted the facts
As historians are quite apt to claim
They say it was London
You know London itself
That caught fire
But it wasn't it was Tom's little game

Marlborough Street caught fire
So did Vine Street
In fact the whole orange set
And the flames turned right at Free Parking
And burnt the red one, whose name I forget
You know the red one to the right of the car park

Worth eight sovs with an hotel
Well that one whatever it's called caught fire
And so did Mayfair as well

Tom's little game was one ball of flame
Whilst he was out watching the birds
Community Chest
The whole pile of cards caught fire
Obliterating the words
When he went back to work then he noticed
His game was reduced to a cinder
And not thinking what the outcome would be
He tossed it out of the window
 Out went the game into Pudding Lane
It landed in the road in a heap
Passers by thought 'Oooh, a barbecue'
So they tossed on some pigs and some sheep
Up went the flames into Pudding Lane
The Monument nearly caught fire
They threw on more meat
For people to eat
And the flames grew higher and higher

Yes they lost the odd street or two
But it wasn't a Great Fire as such
So they lost London Bridge
So did we to America
But no it wasn't really that much
In Sixteen Hundred and Sixty Six
The Great Fire of London started

Some say it was due to an easterly wind
Others say Samuel Pepys farted

But I tell you now
It was none of those things
It was Tom's Monopoly board
When the flames turned right at Free Parking
And burnt the red one
Whatever it's called

      They say that small can be beautiful and that is exactly how I feel about The Monument. There are so many things to see in London, including modern attractions such as The London Eye, along with huge buildings such as The Houses of Parliament and Westminster Abbey, where poets apparently get plastered into the walls when they snuff it, plus a few composers that have become decomposers, but I find it such a shame that few take in the small column that tells such a huge story relating to the history of London. On the very spot where we stood London fell to its knees, engulfed by flames, yet it rose from the ashes and became what it is today. Quite remarkable. It's top of the list for me, and now hopefully you too, followed by the vaults of The Houses of Parliament where they found Guy Fawkes hiding. Ah yes, dear old Guy Fawkes, the man who gave us bonfire night and frightened pets. Only in Britain can we celebrate a total failure, something that never actually happened, every year on November 5th. Yes, only in Britain.

To complete this story it was only in more recent times that I discovered Sir Christopher Wren came from just down the road to where I live now in Salisbury. He was born in East Knoyle, a small village on the road to Sherborne. I've driven through the village many times and there are no signs of amazing monuments anywhere, which leaves me to assume he wasn't much of an architect when he was a little boy. Things must have picked up for him when he was given his first geometry set by his mum, or when he had left school and started work.

Connecting somehow with the evils of 2020, The Great Plague, just before The Great Fire of London, was the last bubonic plague in Britain and it killed over 100,000 people. Have you ever wondered what they did with all those dead bodies? It's all a tad macabre, I know that, but it's interesting, nonetheless. They buried them and the graves stretched for miles out towards the east of London, and thus became the name of Gravesend in Kent. Just imagine them trying to dig graves through the foundations of that Dartford Tunnel. Yes, those early artisans were clever alright. That's because they studies reference books instead of messing around all day on their mobile phones.

Chapter Six – Gerald Ford

Gerald Ford was the 38th President of The United States of America, serving from 1974 to 1977 and you are about to meet him. Now I fully accept he doesn't really rank alongside Abraham Lincoln or John F Kennedy, but he was a President nonetheless, and so quite an important bloke. If you are interested, and I'm sure you're not, he was the only boy scout to ascend to the Presidency of The United States. Wow, we sat round fires and sang Kumbaya never wanting to become politicians. One of my dreads during my early years was that they would find another verse to that boring song that lasted an eternity anyway with no need of an extension. Someone's bunjee-jumping Lord, Kumbaya.

Once again, this is an experience I enjoyed whilst on my own. You should have been there.

We have just played at The Cellar Door in Washington and are about to move on to Denver, Colorado to support Esther Phillips, so we just have to visit The White House before we go. I love British history, but my knowledge of American history is not too strong. My previous home in Hampshire was older that America, and quite possibly more interesting as it was made from old ship's beams that were cut down in The New Forest the very same forest from where they acquired logs to build the ships that sailed to America. The time has come to show some interest in America and take in part of its glory.

There's nothing too surprising about The White House. It's a big house and it's white. We're not talking Buckingham Palace here, but even so it is a place to see with our own eyes while we are stranded in the land of liberty.

The site where we both stand was selected in 1791 by America's first President, George Washington. Strangely, The White House was actually designed by an Irishman by the name of James Hoban and not an American. The place took eight years to build. I wonder if a whole year of those eight was spent staring at colour-charts? Shall we go for white after all? The first President to live there was John Adams.

So, there you go, that's the history behind the place and we are right there. We enter into the gardens through two massive wrought-iron gates and we slowly meander across the manicured lawns. It was allowed back then in the 1970s. I never ever carried a camera with me and this day is no exception, preferring to enjoy the moment in real time.

As we walk along one of the pathways we see a gentleman coming the other way. He's important because some tourists are saluting him and he is responding in a similar fashion. Maybe he isn't that important, we're not sure because, after all, he only has one guy walking with him, not an entourage of dodgy looking men in black suits and sunglasses, no, just the one man in white shirt and tie. Imagine that happening today? If only some would say.

The President of The United States, Gerald Ford, breaks from his walk and comes across to shake our hands. There are about a dozen of us in all and we wait on the end because, in total honestly, we're not even too sure who he is. He looks a bit like Bruce Willis what with his swept back hairstyle. Our quizzical minds are laid to rest when one of the crowd call him Mr. President.

Yes, it really is Gerald Ford. He shakes your hand and asks you if you're having a nice day and when you reply he realises you have an English accent. He raises his eyebrows in interest and asks what we are doing in his country and you tell him we have just done a gig at The Cellar Door. President Ford knew the place and had been there himself, which catches you unawares. You are even more aghast when he uses the term 'gig' himself too. Now that's what you call a super-cool President. Mind you, Bill Clinton played the saxophone when he wasn't doing other things that required a similar motion.

President Ford wishes us both well and continues on his way. Nice man, friendly man. I suppose, thinking back, it was no big deal, but you can boast you met a President, not just shaking their hand but enjoying a short chat with him too. How many people have enjoyed such a moment? I'm sure we can both think of another American President we wouldn't want to meet in a month of Sundays, thank you very much.

Once again, that chance meeting inspired a poem, such is my way. At least you now know how this poem came to be, because you were there, second time around.

Of all the things that happened at sea
Two in particular have made history
The Titanic, when she slipped into the drink
And everyone said she just couldn't sink
The band played on regardless it's said
In bow ties and inflatable vests
The captain requested they take to the boats
But the band said 'We don't do requests'

Now let's go back a century or two
To the days our great, great grandfathers knew
To Fourteen Hundred and Ninety Two
When Columbus took his new boat out
He only intended to sail for the day
To take his mates on a trip round the bay
But his compass broke and he went the wrong way
To a land no-one had heard of

He was known as an unpredictable bloke
So his pals thought he'd set them a practical joke
But by the time baby sitters were paid they'd be broke
And their hands would be blistered from rowing
Billy Brown was one of Columbus' crew
In fact he was half, there were only the two
Him and Jim Johnson who Columbus knew

For he'd a seat next to him at the Arsenal
After a few months on the ocean had passed
Poor Billy Brown had been strapped to the mast
Spying for land through a magnifying glass
Which he used for pulling out splinters
They must have been smelly and cold I suppose
For a trip round the bay they'd not packed change of clothes
And that must have got up the Indians nose
When they landed three months or so later

They anchored and swam to the shore in the dark
Poor Billy Brown was attacked by a shark
His body was covered in unsightly marks
Except for his legs…..they had gone
Christopher's geography wasn't too strong
So when he whiffed a strange hamburger pong
And some stroppy tennis star carrying on
He said 'I shall name this the land of my merry fathers'
Billy Brown said 'That's sounds silly to me
A merry old chap though your father may be
Your Father's called Colin and quite honestly
Colin's a very strange name for a Country'
Columbus said 'Colin's the name I have chose
So we best go tell them over there I suppose
Last one down to that hot dog stand goes'
Billy with no legs was well lumbered

He went to the Indians gave them the news
'His merry Father's name we shall use

Though Colin isn't the name I would choose
I name this new land....a merry Co......'
But before the word Colin could fall from his tongue
You'll never believe what the Indians had done
They chopped off his head..... Billy looked glum
His best hat had dropped in the water
"A merry Co..." Columbus spat
"A merry Co..." I'm turning down flat
"A merry Co...What sort of name is that?
I still wish to call this land Colin."
So what if things hadn't turned out that way
What if the Titanic hadn't sunk on that day?
But Columbus' boat had....there'd be no US of A
What if things had been different?

No Bourbon to get us all as drunk as newts
No Monopoly Board or Trivial Pursuits
We'd have words like jam and wouldn't use jelly
No more American soaps on the telly
But alas great sadness would be felt in our house
Imagine no Popeye or no Mickey Mouse
So thank you Christopher Billy as well
For life without that lot around would be hell
On behalf of my daughter thank you for going
And thanks to your crew for three months of rowing
Words cannot express how grateful I am
You did us all proud..... thank you Uncle Sam

Chapter Seven – Joni Mitchell

When I worked as a radio presenter at Capital Radio I got the chance to meet so many great musicians. None greater than the wonderful, glorious Joni Mitchell, one of my favourite-ever songwriters. It was in 1981. Imagine being by my side on this amazing day. I've told this story on many occasions, but on this occasion it takes on a different because you are meeting her too. Oh yes, you should have been there.

Before you joined me I was staring at a noticeboard in the cafeteria at Capital and as I sat having a cup of tea with fellow presenter, Mike Smith, I noticed Joni was coming in for an interview. We had to put our names down for interviews of forthcoming guests we fancied chatting to and I was amazed nobody had volunteered to interview her, the legend that was Joni Mitchell, so I leapt at the chance. I rate it as one of the highlights of my radio career, hang on, let's say the ultimate highlight because there was nothing greater. I've invited you to join me as I return to that day in January 1981 and I bet you cannot wait to come back with me right now.

As we meet her, the first thing that strikes us is her diminutive height. She is so tiny and slight in stature, oh and she's also a chain-smoker, something that really takes both us both by surprise. That beautiful pure voice, you would never have thought it would you? She is wearing a yellow floral dress and a leather jacket. On her feet are a battered old pair of trainers, confirming she is a tried and tested folkie who doesn't give a dam about fashion. I immediately fall in love with Joni Mitchell and you do too. Meeting such an incredible person is a rare happening in life and something we will remember for the rest of our lives. We both shake her gentle hand and take her up to Studio 2, another small interview studio with a round table and four chairs, with little room for anything else. I have my notes in my hand and I can't wait to get stuck in.

Joni is in London to plug her new album along with her forthcoming concert at The Royal Festival Hall. We begin to talk as Joni lights up yet another cigarette. It was acceptable to smoke in a studio in those days and she made the most of it.

I switch on the Studer recording machine and we are in business.

Having plugged the Festival Hall gig, I then ask her about her guitar playing;

'Joni, before you go, I'd love to know how you came up with the idea of tuning your guitar to an open G chord, thus giving you that unique sound on your Clouds album.'

Joni stares at us both and I can tell immediately that she has been asked something far more interesting than the usual questions during the treadmill of record and concert plugs demanded by her record company. She giggles slightly as she stubs out her fag and tells how the question makes such a nice change from the usual round of uninspired questions she is expected to answer with great enthusiasm. I explain that I play the guitar myself and was indeed inspired by the technique she used on that iconic album, so she proceeds to tell us the whole story, guitarist to guitarist, and dare I say she loves telling me.

Let's just take stock here, we are talking around a table to the one and only Joni Mitchell, the most famous and respected female songwriter and guitarist in the whole world, and yet she looks so tiny and vulnerable. It makes me feel very special in a strange way and for her it is obviously something beyond the drudgery, meeting a couple of fans with far more interest than she had expected. She continues her explanation and we are both fascinated and captivated. Joni seems to be enjoying it too if I'm brutally honest and if you will forgive the arrogance.

At the age of 9, she tells us she contracted polio and this affected the use of her hands and with such a weakness she changed her guitar style to accommodate her unfortunate condition. Strangely she also boasts to having started smoking at the age of 9 too and burst into hysterics at such an admission.

We speak for ages about guitar styles, once she discovers I'm a folkie like her and not just some boring radio presenter. Like me she started out on the folk scene, not in London, but in Alberta, Canada, under her real name of Roberta Anderson. We have so little in common and yet so much in common if you see what I mean.

'Joni, I find it odd you had a huge hit with Woodstock even though you weren't there.'

She giggled again like a naughty schoolgirl.

'I wrote it for someone who was there.'

I assume, and still assume, she meant Graham Nash who left The Hollies to become part of Crosby, Stills and Nash but I do not press the issue as it really is none of my business unless she chooses to expand further, something she chooses not to do.

It's the end of the interview and she thanks us for being so interested in her career and I tell her the pleasure has been all ours. My god, there is so much more to Joni Mitchell than Big Yellow Taxi, such a brilliant songwriter, artist and poet.

She has a schedule to meet because other radio stations have lined up interviews too but, out of courtesy, I offer her a cup of coffee before she sets off and against all the odds she agrees. In my hand, as I leave the studio, I have an Ampex 456 reel-to-reel tape bursting with remarkable footage of a remarkable woman. I ask you to look after the tape in an insignificant grey box and we head off to the cafeteria. We pass members of staff coming the other way and I would give anything to tell them we are going for a coffee with one of the greatest females that have ever set foot in the world of music. They are oblivious as I lead the way with such a tiny woman walking behind me, not even coming up to my shoulder, as you ask her if she's enjoying her stay in London. It's so damn surreal isn't it? You should have been there the first time round.

Joni chooses iced water and passes on the offer of a sandwich or a piece of cake and she compliments me on my homework as she sits and signs each page of my notes with a pencil that has seen better days. She passes one of the signatures to you and you have a souvenir that you will cherish forever. The ironic thing is I never glanced at my notes once, I didn't need to as I knew so much about her, so they ended up as nothing more than a very special autograph book.

It's time to go our separate ways but she invites us to her Royal Festival Hall concert and we go backstage and meet her for a second time, such a thrill and such an honour. She even remembers our names which is highly impressive.

I love Joni Mitchell. I have always loved Joni Mitchell and this event is one of the greatest of my music career.

As I said, I've always loved her music and, although not in her league by any stretch of the imagination, I compare my career path with hers as a songwriter, poet and artist. Please don't get me wrong, as I said she is incomparable, but I took the same path just the same. I could never write songs as good as hers, or poems either, and my paintings have never been anything near her skills, but it was a similar route I took and I bet we both shared equal amounts of loneliness that comes with such a craving to be creative. I hope you enjoyed meeting her as much as I did.

One of the guests on my ITV Saturday night show a few years later was Marc Cohn who composed and had a huge hit with Walking in Memphis. During a coffee break at rehearsals at The London Studios I told Marc, a massive Joni fan himself, the story of how we had interviewed Joni just down the road and he was highly impressed.

'Richard, you met Joni Mitchell?'

'I certainly did.'

'I'm so envious of you, man.'

Hey, I'd just met Marc Cohn and that was quite something too.

During the afternoon rehearsal Marc was fiddling around on the grand piano as the crew were sorting their camera angles and I joined him on my acoustic guitar. We busked an impromptu version of Case of You, my favourite Joni Mitchell song of all time. We decided to do it during the evening recording and I loved every minute of it. Unfortunately, the editor sent it, unceremoniously, to the cutting-room floor and our efforts never saw the light of day. Oh well, Marc sang Walking in Memphis on my show and it reached the top twenty by the Monday morning, just two days later, such was the power of television when there were only four channels. Nice guy, nice song, nice story.

> I've looked at clouds from both sides now.
> It was such a celebration
> You were such an inspiration
> To spend some time with you

Even just an hour or two

Another very interesting fact that Joni told me during our interview was how difficult it was to perform in Canada, as musicians had to pay a 200-dollar union fee. Sometimes musician unions can take away work from those who are their members, which is very strange. Her most popular song 'Both Sides Now' has been recorded by 1,200 different artists and yet she struggled to scrape the money together to get herself started in the music business due to the union demands. It's a strange world out there. Musicians of today trying to make headway in such a topsy-turvy world would never be in a position to raise such cash just to keep legal. I don't think they'd even bother.

As for my good mate Mike Smith who was sitting next to me when I noticed Joni's name on the noticeboard, he survived a helicopter crash in 1988 but sadly died in 2014 at just 59 years of age during major heart surgery. Yes he has to be in the conclusion of this story as he did indeed sit beside me in the cafeteria drinking coffee as I noticed that memo that said Joni Mitchell was coming to town. He remained in his chair at the table while I jumped up and scribbled my name on the noticeboard. We also went to radio school together.

Smithy and I laughed so many times as we made our way through the years at Capital Radio and out the other side. He became a national figure on BBC Radio One and TV too, hosting the That's Entertainment TV series, not bad for some who was once Noel Edmunds's driver, both coming from Romford in Essex. I didn't make Radio One myself, I had no real desire to if I'm honest, but I interviewed Joni Mitchell and that's good enough for me. Hang on, we interviewed Joni Mitchell. Such a spectacular day, just imagine the three of us sitting around that table in deep conversation with such a genius. During my years at Capital Radio I obviously undertook numerous interviews but no others would have licked the boots of that one.

Chapter Eight – The Battle Of New Orleans

I am about to travel to New Orleans, a musician's dream journey if ever there was one. It's the home of the blues and ragtime music that has influenced so many great musicians over the last one hundred and fifty years. You can be just as excited as me if you take your seat on the plane next to me.

We're travelling business class thanks to the generosity of Production Plus, the corporate entertainment company that have booked me. We sit back and relax as the plane takes to the air. It's a 12 hour flight from Heathrow and you happen to be sitting next to one of the world's worst fliers. As I always say, if God had wanted us to fly he would have given us tickets, so don't expect too much lucid conversation as we crash through the rainclouds of England in an attempt to reach the clear blue sky above. I'm gripping the arms of my seat so hard my knuckles have turned white and you are smiling at my misfortune.

After a movie I can't remember, copious amounts of gin and tonic and a few sleeps on the way we arrive in New Orleans. The heat hits us, the same heat you feel when you take roast potatoes out of the oven. We're way down in the state of Louisiana in a city built on the banks of The Mississippi River. You may have thought you've seen some wide rivers in your time but this big boy takes the biscuit. On its way down to The Gulf of Mexico it is 11 miles wide at its widest point, that wider than the city of London for heaven's sake. It definitely beats any watery vein that weaves through Great Britain, particularly the one that runs past the bottom of my garden in Salisbury, no comparison.

We have two days to kill before the corporate show, so we take in all the tourist sites such as Bourbon Street where the much celebrated Mardi Gras takes place and we visit the home of Tennessee Williams who wrote A Streetcar Named Desire. From the French Quarter, where all the well-known sites are situated, we turn left on the main drag that takes us down to the mighty river. There is an amazing shopping mall beside the river and we take a stroll around the various shops within that sell endless memorabilia of those wonderful days of jazz and the blues. It's odd so much money is made from so many poverty-stricken musicians, but that's the way it is and the way it was. We get it and we decide it's a case of gone but not forgotten.

At the end of the shopping mall is a bar with a balcony and we are enjoying a lunchtime drink when we suddenly hear music filling the air. It's a pipe-organ approaching, belting out Alexander's Ragtime Band, and before we know it this huge paddle-steamer of monumental proportions is preparing to end its journey just down the river from where we are sitting. We decide to take a closer look and we can see through the windows that it resembles a kind of posh cowboy saloon of years gone by. By the booking office is a sign that invites us to take a two-hour trip on The Natchez, this big white cowboy town on water with a huge red paddle on the back. It is offering a trip to the scene of The

Battle of New Orleans and me, forever into my history, decide it's something that has to be done, even though we lost.

The Battle of New Orleans took place on 8th January, 1815 and was made famous to us Brits by the song that was a big hit years ago for the skiffler Lonnie Donegan.

1814 we took a little trip
Along with Colonel Jackson down the mighty Mississip'
We took a little bacon and we took a little beans
And we caught the bloody British in the town of New Orleans

We fired our guns and the British kept a-comin'
There wasn't as many as there was a while ago
We fired once more and they began to runnin'
On down the Mississippi to the Gulf of Mexico

We looked down a river and we see'd the British come
And there must have been a hundred of 'em beatin' on the drum
They stepped so high and they made their bugles ring
We stood behind our cotton bales and didn't say a thing

We fired our guns and the British kept a-comin'
There wasn't as many as there was a while ago
We fired once more and they began to runnin'
On down the Mississippi to the Gulf of Mexico

The British army decided to take on the Americans and yes, we definitely lost, with dreadful casualties, but hey we got a good song out of it so there was an upside. This really is a trip I just didn't want to do on my own, thus this invitation.

To go to the actual battlefield, five miles from the city, is a mouth-watering thought as we climb aboard The Natchez. There's a traditional jazz-band bashing out all the old standards as we sit down, riverbank side, on a deck beside an open-air bar. There is a loud blast that nearly perforates our ear-drums and the big red paddle begins to turn, churning up the muddy waters of The Mississippi and we are on our way up the river to where it all happened. Fancy a hot-dog? Why not? I have no idea what they make the sauce out of, but it isn't tomato ketchup and it burns the back of my throat but some bonfire in full throttle.

After about an hour the steamer moors up at a levy, the very same thing that Don McLean said was dry in American Pie, and we then disembark and walk to the battlefield itself. It's all so calm and difficult to imagine such a bloodthirsty event took place there at a cost of so many lives.

We study the map that shows where various skirmishes took place and we realise we are standing exactly where the Highlanders came a right cropper against the twenty gun American batteries. How much blood must have seeped into the ground on which we stood? It didn't bare thinking about as we looked around at the tranquillity and peace. It's fair to say the Americans haven't won every battle they got involved with but they won this one.

At the gift shop, which probably wasn't there when the fighting was going on, we both buy a genuine musket shot, a small cannonball, that had been dredged out from the river. Blimey, the guy that fired my one must have been a really bad shot. There were thousands upon thousands of them dredged up apparently and we both laughed at the fact that at least we were both buying one that hadn't killed anyone. They are mounted on beautiful wooden plinths that bore the inscription 'a musket ball from The Battle of New Orleans, 1815.' They look classy, a cut way above those plastic policeman helmets that tourists buy at The Tower of London.

Although we are doing a gig the day after tomorrow we are having great fun playing at being tourists, so much so that we decide to go on another excursion the following day. Talk about chalk and cheese. We are off down the Louisiana Swamps to take a flat-bottom boat down the watery veins that are infested with alligators. Oh well, it has to be done. Frightening? You should have been there.

The boat is much smaller than we anticipated and I make the point that any decent-sized alligator could bite the thing in half with ease. You don't look too sure as the little craft sets off through the bright-green water, really bright-green luminous water, to where the alligators are hanging out awaiting our arrival. They must see these boats a dozen times a day and so they are obviously prepared for the human invasion of their territory. In the blazing heat we wind our way through the maze of watery inlets no wider than a small British canal, until we reach a clearing. The engine, that sounds like nothing more than something that drives a garden lawnmower, grinds to a halt and all falls silent. Suddenly, we are totally surrounded by these curious reptiles, their snouts rising above the water and more or less spitting water at us with a certain amount of disdain. They don't look too friendly, but we have no need to worry so long as we don't fall in. And I paid good money for this near-death experience. We both need our heads testing, but I know that anyway.

The man steering the boat, I hasten to call him the captain as he looks more like some hobo who should be strumming a banjo on a porch, tells us all it's feeding time and he hands out sticks, broken tree branches actually, to all twelve of us on his boat. The alligators know more than we do as they move in closer, tapping the side of the boat with their snouts. Was it Robert Browning who said 'Oh to be in England now that Spring is here' somewhere in his home thoughts from abroad? At this very moment neither of us could have agreed more. What the hell are we doing?

The nutcase boat-owner sticks a marshmallow on the end of his stick and suddenly an alligator leaps out of the water like some not so graceful salmon heading upstream. All twelve of us are startled to say the least and then he passes a marshmallow to each of us. You're not so sure about this and neither am I. I've done some stupid things in my time but this ranks very high up the list. The alligators are impatient little buggers and they splash about as we prepare to load marshmallows on the end of our sticks and offer them their lunch. Your stick bends as one of them leaps up and steals your offering before being chased by another half a dozen of the beasts that want a bite of his bounty. We are all laughing, laughing very nervously, but laughing just the same. I've never been a fan of alligators and the whole occasion didn't make me change my opinion of them. It was one of those trips that was enjoyable and yet a relief it had come to an end as the alligators disappeared in the distance, full of sugar that couldn't have been that great for their digestive systems. I have to say I don't think I would have been that good for their digestive systems either so it was best for both parties that I didn't fall in the water after all. Ah, that luminous green water gets more vivid every time I tell this story. Pea soup describes it the best.

  I don't remember too much about the gig the following day and it's hardly surprising considering all that had happened the two days before. All I recall was that it was a show for IBM and I supported a tribute ABBA band from Australia. Corporate gigs always seemed to take me to places I would otherwise never have visited in my life, so I rarely turned them down, even though I hated flying to them

  And so it was time to wave goodbye to New Orleans. You can keep your alligators thank you very much. Our army never won the battle there but I'm sure that was a good thing considering what was on offer in the Louisiana countryside if they had hung around long enough to find out. Give me the pretty lanes of Wiltshire any time. There's no cannonballs or musket shot buried here but there's a god few Roman coins still rolling about in the dirt. Now that, dear America, is what really did call history.

Chapter Nine – World Cup Winner

Gordon Banks, Ray Wilson and George Cohen
Nobby Stiles and Alan Ball
Roger Hunt, Jack and Bobby Charlton
Schoolboy heroes one and all
Hurst and Peters scored the winners
And the cup was Bobby Moore's
That was how we beat the Germans
One World Cup and two World Wars

Much of my childhood was spent kicking a football around on my own in a park near to where I lived in East Ham. Something happened one day, a chance meeting, that I'd love to have shared, even if it was so my young mates would have believed me. You should have been there.

I loved my football when I was a kid, with dreams to become a professional player when I left school, but let me stress before we go any further that you don't need to be a football nut like me to have thoroughly enjoyed being by my side on this one. It was a very special day when I met a very special person.

We're off to the East End of London and we're travelling back to the late 1950s. Barking Road is one of two major spines that run through the East End, the other being Whitechapel Road. On its way to what is now the M25 motorway there is a right turn just before The Duke's Head pub as it used to be. It's called Park Avenue and it turns into Folkestone Road just before it links into Blaney Crescent where I used to live with my mum and dad. If you take that road, with its varying names, as far as it goes, you arrive at Gooseley Park and that's where I'm inviting you to join me as I kick a ball around on my own pretending to be Bobby Charlton or someone similar. If you continue through the park and out the other side you would eventually end up in the River Thames at Woolwich so be careful. It isn't luminous green like The Mississippi but it's most unpleasant just the same.

    It's nice to have someone playing alongside me for a change as you've joined me and we're having a great time scoring goals and making great saves, until our kickaround is momentarily ended when an unkempt grey car draws up by the park railings and out steps a young, blonde man. He folds his arms and leans against the car door and gestures for us to carry on playing, attracted by the West Ham shirt my mum had bought me for Christmas. You try to dribble past me and I beat you with a tackle that would nowadays lead to a red card and possible imprisonment the way footballers roll around on the ground when they trip over an ant. The man claps my attempt, walks towards us and joins in. We play one-touch football and it is amazing to watch a man with such magical feet. We try to get the ball from him but he just laughs quietly as he uses all the tricks in the book to beat off our attempts. After half an hour or so the session ends and we sit cross-legged on the grass. He asks if I am a West Ham supporter and I tell him yes, born and bred, and that I have a dream of playing for them one day. The man goes to his car and produces a pair of claret-coloured socks with sky blue turnovers, telling me they are genuine West Ham socks that I may well wear when I am older if I make the grade. He told us his name, a name neither of us shall ever forget, Bobby Moore.

As he leaves us he doesn't shake our hands, but simply pats us both on the head before heading off down the road to Barking where he lived.

That nice man in Gooseley Park became captain of both West Ham and England and he lifted The World Cup in 1966. How does it feel to have had a kickaround with the greatest defender the football world has ever seen? Ha, no wonder you couldn't get the ball off him. It really is something to tell the grandchildren, if they will believe you.

When his playing days ended the great Bobby Moore joined Capital Radio as a football pundit and our paths crossed many times. I found him to be a painfully shy man and I often wonder if that's what made him join in with a youngster kicking a ball around in the park on his own, that is until you came along and joined in. Did you ever dream about becoming an England international after meeting Bobby Moore? I most certainly did;

I wish I'd played for England like you did.
I wish I'd been a quarter good as you.
I was useless and I knew in my claret and my blue
but it doesn't mean I didn't want to be an international.

I've said it all before, I wish I'd been Bobby Moore
How I wish I had had his skill.
Yes I've said it all before, I wish I'd been Bobby Moore
but I never was and never ever will.

I had no choice but remain a back-street international with a dream that was bound to fade and die like those bubbles West Ham fans sing about.

I'm just eleven but I'm not stupid
My feet are firm on the ground
I was born on the wrong side of London
To see the sun shining down
But at least I have my dreams
And some people don't know what that means
So don't pity my bashed about shoes
I can be anyone that I choose

I'm an international
And that's all I want to be
I'm an international
And that's good enough for me
I'm a back street international

I'm just eleven but I'm not stupid
I know I'll never make the grade
I know I have more chance of climbing a mountain
Or making it in the hit parade
But at least I have my dreams
I can play for all the winning teams

I know they will have to wait a while
But some day they will marvel at my style

I'm an international
And that's all I want to be
I'm an international
And that's good enough for me
I'm a back street international

I'm just eleven but I'm not stupid
For an hour every night after school
And an hour before assembly
This back yard is my Wembley
I've sure hit some girls against this wall
But I know I'm running out of time
This could be the end of the line
The big time is a million miles away
But I scored for England today

I'm an international
And that's all I want to be
I'm an international
And that's good enough for me
I'm a back street international

I'm just eleven but I'm not stupid
My feet are firm on the ground
I was born on the wrong side of London
To see the sun shining down
But at least I have my dreams

And some people don't know what that means
So don't pity my bashed about shoes
I can be anyone that I choose

I'm an international
And that's all I want to be
I'm an international
And that's good enough for me
I'm a back street international

Chapter Ten – My Recording Studio

I spend endless hours in my own recording studio in Salisbury. Over 50 years I have been in and out of studios more times than I can count, going way back to 1968 when I went into such a sacred place for the very first time. It was called the Livingston Studios in Barnet, run by a guy called Nic Kinsey and it was the highlight of my musical life up to that point.

Recording in my own studio is a solitary time when I can just be myself and not worry what's going on in the big, bad world outside. It certainly helped me get through the 2020 crisis that befell us all. I love being on my own in there, but I know there is a certain mystique for those who have never set foot in such a place. Many people wonder how records or soundtracks for television and radio are made so I'm going to take you into mine for a while and show you how such recordings come about. It's what I would call simple but effective recording. It's all changed so much since the days when singers would crowd around a microphone and record as if they were on stage. That doesn't happen much these days.

I'm nothing more than a singer/songwriter so my own recording techniques are relatively simple, but I think you'll still find it interesting.

So, it's 10am in the morning, so definitely no singing until later in the day when the vocal chords can take such a bashing. I have a song ready to record and I start from the beginning by recording a metronome onto track 1. Once the guitar has been recorded I will dispense with it so it doesn't matter much about the quality as it's simply to keep time.

As my production assistant you sit beside me at the mixing desk and press the play and record buttons at the same time and away we go, recording a metronome from my keyboard. It isn't exactly inspiring, but it's an important factor as most singers tend to speed up during a song and so it will hold me back and keep me in time, like reins on a horse.

The second part of the session is to record my guitar, no voice, just my guitar. Although my guitar is an acoustic Martin D28 it has the electrics inside that allow me to record into a desk, either on stage or in the recording studio. This is called DI or direct injection, and to do this we need to switch the recording machine to phantom power, a boost for the signal, as my guitar, or any acoustic guitar for that matter, doesn't really give the kind of signal required for either performance or recording.

To get the signal from my guitar to the desk with its phantom power we use what's known as the aforementioned DI Box, the small metallic box you would have probably often see guitarists use on stage. The guitar lead is plugged into the input socket and a lead from the output goes into track 2 on the recording machine. Whilst I play the guitar you watch the signal on the machine through LEDs that show you if the playing is being recorded at too high a level. Then you press the record button, as before, and off we go again.

Track 2 is recorded and saved and finalised on the computer.

I'm now about to record another guitar on top of what I've just recorded. Because we recorded the first guitar straight onto the machine through the DI box we don't need to wear headphones as we are not using microphones as yet and so I can play along by listening through the speakers. The second guitar is now recorded and saved and we can keep the two guitars isolated or bounce them together onto track 4. It's up to us really. The guitar work is done and it's time to have a cup of tea before we start on the vocals. That's when a production assistant such as yourself really comes into their own, becoming almost indispensable. Forget all that glycerine and honey stuff, a nice cup of tea and a couple of rich tea biscuits will do me fine thanks. Just so you know, a second cup of tea will make me sing even better.

We record the voice onto track 5, this time using headphones as the guitars in the speakers will be heard on the vocal track and once this has been done and we are happy with the vocals we let the machine do the work for us. You 'bounce' or double-track my voice to another channel and this effectively increases the power of my vocals, in my case making me sound much better than what I actually am, which isn't that difficult. So, we have two guitars and effectively two voices saved onto the computer

As production assistant you have noted what went onto what track, only 5 on this particular basic session but it can get complicated when 20 or 30 tracks are being laid down on just one song. We both agree we can hear both the vocals and the singing was passable and so we add a touch of reverb and fiddle around with the EQ, that's what you do with a good old fashioned stereo that has bass, middle and treble.

We mix the guitar and vocal together, deleting the metronome on track 1 as it's no longer needed. Once happy to master by writing the track to the on-board computer and finalizing onto MP3 or CD, whichever we have decided.

Whatever we add is again through direct-injection and with the luxury of a digital machine we can add as many tracks as we wish. And to think George Martin recorded The Beatles Magical Mystery Tour album on just four tracks, two of which were Ringo's drums. That man really was a genius in every sense of the word.

We make a CD copy to place on the shelf, even though everything is saved onto the computer. Don't forget I'm of the old school and I trust computers as far as I can throw the, and, believe me, I've thrown a few in my time out of sheer frustration. I loved the reel to reel tapes and my huge, old analog mixing desk, but it just isn't like that anymore. At least digital recording gives you more space.

That's basically it, you've been in my recording studio with me and pressed a few buttons so you are now a fully-fledged assistant producer, or assistant sound engineer, whichever you choose to call yourself.

Nothing much but I hope you enjoyed me putting you through your technical paces.

For many who have recorded in a studio before, with far more proficiency than I can offer myself, this chapter means absolutely nothing. I get that, but for you, coming in for the first time, it was a basic insight into how we operate in the confines of a digital recording studio. It isn't rocket science.

Chapter Eleven – Knebworth

The Knebworth Festival took place for the first time on July 20, 1974, headlined by The Allman Brothers and The Doobie Brothers. In the years that followed the names that played there was a phenomenal list including The Rolling Stones, Pink Floyd, Queen, Oasis and many many more.

On June 21, 1980, I played there too and I was wondering if you would like to join me, come backstage and meet the other acts on the bill and have a nice day out in the countryside.

So who are you about to meet? The Beach Boys, Mike Oldfield and Santana. Does that interest you? It all sounds fairly idyllic does it not? A summer festival in the middle of summer in a beautiful part of the country. Hang on, this is England we are talking about and not America. The weather is downright appalling, so much so that I'm surprised they didn't add Noah to the line-up. It has chucked it down for most of the day and the field has turned into a mud bath as a quarter of a million festival-goers try to stand up straight without sliding over. Ah, good old English weather, always guaranteed to let you down. At least there may well be a heatwave on Christmas Day this year.

The A1 is bumper to bumper with cars as far back as Stevenage as we make our way to an artist's entrance that luckily remained a secret and therefore not so congested. We have our own car-park too and our very own mobile home dressing room, so the rain isn't as bad for us.

In the tea-tent we meet up with some of my old mates and it's a jovial atmosphere, that 'the show must go on' kind of bulldog attitude. You are introduced to Alan Hull, the lead singer of Lindisfarne and someone I bumped into regularly when he was on the folk scene. He's a quiet man with a strong Geordie accent but don't be fooled because this man had a heart of steel and we chat about the last gig we did together at Lewisham Concert Hall. It's a nice feeling of two old work-buddies enjoying a reunion.

All the bands who are on early in the afternoon have arrived and relaxing as their respective road crews push huge flight cases of equipment up a giant ramp at the back of the stage. They're not helped by the weather, of course, but they get there, each of them puffing and panting in celebration of reaching the top, as though they have just conquered Everest.

Roadies are roadies, a breed apart and they all look the same with their pony-tails, black tee-shirts and shorts with bunches of tools hanging from their belts. They never socialise with you as they are far too busy, but it's great for you to see them busying away like bees around a honeypot, all of them knowing exactly what they are doing.

In a couple of hours the back of the stage is stacked with those aluminium boxes, amplifiers and black drapes so the view you saw of the empty field earlier has disappeared from sight. It's an amazing transition and the next time you climb the metal stairs with me that lead to the stage there are a quarter of a million faces staring at you, waiting for the show to begin.

It's a busy day for me because I'm performing on stage between each act, so basically I'm performing seven times during the course of the afternoon so I find you a superb vantage point, sitting on a flight case stage left and leave you to your own devices, but also being the closest member of the audience out of the quarter of a million, and the driest too.

I introduce you to Elkie Brooks, a dear friend who I'd toured Britain with for four years. She's with her sound man and husband, Trevor Jordan, a Stevenage boy back on home turf.

Despite the atrocious weather the show begins on time and The Blues Band are revving it up and pleasing the damp crowd. And so it goes on until the rain becomes so heavy and proceedings are halted. It's time to sling Digance on stage again to keep the crowd happy and we perform the loudest version of Singing In The Rain I've ever heard. Spirits are high but there are a few problems behind the scenes.

I'm feeling cold and we decide to go and sit in my car with the heater full on. I'm chilled to the bone and my fingers don't really want to play the guitar. Who says hello and climbs into the back of the car with us? None other than Mike Oldfield who is soon to perform Tubular Bells. Mike and I were on Transatlantic Records together and although history says that Richard Branson gave him his recording break by forming Virgin Records it isn't true. Mike was half of a duo with his sister Sally and they went out as SallyAngie. We talk about old times, both working under Nat Joseph before he takes his leave and wishes us both well.

As darkness falls and the weather abates you are about to enjoy one of the greatest moments of your life. My job is done for the day and so I join you on the side of the stage. We have a pile of towels we have nicked from backstage to make things more comfortable and as we sit there with cups of hot coffee, comfort personified they introduce The Beach Boys. The crowd go mental as suddenly the wet fields of England transform to the West Coast of America and iconic surfing sound fills the air. You have the best seat in the house, no more than three feet away from the legendry Brian Wilson, a true musical genius. Brian hasn't been well for many years but he's on stage just the same, right next to us, leaning on his keyboard as a means of support. A tear comes to my eye and I look over at you and your eyes are behaving equally irresponsibly. We are within touching distance of the man who wrote Good Vibrations, God Only Knows, I Get Around and numerous other titles that could fill the pages of this book. Of course it was a moving experience, one that would never be repeated.

The band are about to perform a song without bass and drums and so drummer Dennis Wilson leaves his kit and wanders over to us and asks for one of the towels we are sitting on. He thanks us and asks how we are doing. It's enough to send shivers down your spine. He's a musical icon.

The interesting little known fact about Dennis Wilson is that he was the only Beach Boy member who actually surfed in real life. Sadly, three years after we met him, Dennis Wilson drowned at the tender age of 39.

So there you have it, a visit backstage with me at The Knebworth Festival. For months afterwards, whenever I did a gig, a few members of the audience would sing out the opening bars to Singing In The Rain. The song didn't quite do for me what it did for Gene Kelly, fair to say, but every time I hear that song or watch that famous film footage I am taken back to that soggy June day in 1980 when I introduced you to Elkie, Mike Oldfield and we chatted to Dennis Wilson of The Beach Boys. It wasn't a bad day really was it?

Chapter Twelve – The Blues Brothers

How many times are you asked to name your favourite film? Me too. Mine is The Blues Brothers starring Dan Aykroyd and John Belushi, with cameo appearances by James Brown, Ray Charles and Aretha Franklin to name but a few. Oh yes, and Twiggy!

It's incredible to think that movie was made over forty years ago, yet it still stands the test of time as a true masterpiece.

It was made in Chicago and that's where we're off to right now. This is such an exciting trip and you'll love every minute. We are on our way to some gigs further down south and our plane has landed in O'Hare International Airport in, yes, Chicago. We hear that, due to bad weather, all inter-connecting flights are cancelled, and so we have a day to kill before continuing on with our journey. I have an idea, a brilliant idea if I may be so arrogant, to find the Triple Rock Church where The Blues Brothers found God, if you know the film. It's where they are enthralled by the pastor, played by James Brown, as he led the service with song and dance. I decide we should go looking for the church where that amazing scene was filmed. Yes, we're off in search of The Triple Rock Church, but we soon discover that such a church never existed. After various searching and questions we discover it was filmed at The Pilgrim Baptist Church, and so we make our way to 9114 South Burley Avenue in south Chicago. We mess up big style because there are two Pilgrim Baptist Churches and we end up going to the wrong one. A taxi that looks more like a black and white police car than a cab takes us to the right one with a driver who tells us he was there in 1980 when they filmed The Blues Brothers. I suppose all cab drivers say that don't they? Interestingly he points out a few other locations as we make our way further south of the city.

When we arrive at the church it takes our breath away. There it is, standing there in all its cinematic glory. It's on a street corner and it's white, bright white if there is such a thing and it's so clean it looks like it was given a fresh coat of paint the day before.

I'm so glad to be here today
Standing outside the Pilgrim Baptist Church
Everybody wants somebody
Everybody wants somebody to love
Someone to love
Someone to kiss
Sometime to miss, now
Someone to squeeze
Someone to please
And I need you you you
I need you you you
I need you you you
I need you you you

The church is much smaller than we both expected. I suppose most Baptist churches are small in comparison to others, but its spire rises up into the sky, good and proud. The whole thing looks like a huge wooden model kit that's been painted white.

How ironic it that 2020 would have seen the 40th Anniversary celebrations at the church, had things been oh so different around the world. The celebration was to include gospel music, a viewing of the movie and a silent auction featuring 21 panels of stained glass, including three that were illuminated by heavenly rays of light in the movie.

As we enter the church we are confronted by a merchandise stall that sells anything Blues Brothers. Tee-shirts, shoulder bags, sunglasses, pork-pie hats, bootlace ties, jeans jackets, just about anything you can think of. To the right is a refreshment area that sells coffee and rock cakes, so we load ourselves up and make our way up the stairs to the gallery to look down on what was cinematic history. It being my favourite film of all time I am overcome to a degree and I sit in silence. You ask me if I'm ok, yes of course I'm fine but I'm completely lost in the awe and splendour of it all.

The front wooden balustrade in the gallery is low but there are little shelves on which to place our cups while we just sit back and take it all in. Hey, this where James Brown sang and Belushi and Aykroyd danced. Talk about me being in my element.

On the way back to the hotel I tell you it has been one of the greatest moments of my life and you can see in my eyes that I mean it. It truly was. We caught our interconnecting flight down south and I said goodbye to The Blues Brothers. John Belushi was born in Chicago just two weeks before I was born in East Ham, but sadly his lifestyle took him from us at the ridiculously young age of 33. Dan Aykroyd, who is actually Canadian and not from Chicago at all, went on to enjoy an illustrious film career in so many aspects of the profession. Yet my mind goes back to John Belushi, a genius of an actor, comedian too in his earlier days, who died just over two years after they made that epic movie. The truth of the matter is that The Blues Brothers will never die, not in my mind anyway and I'm so pleased I could take you to Chicago to share such emotions first hand. Respect to you John Belushi, and in the words of Aretha Franklin;

What you want
Baby, I got it
What you need
Do you know I got it?
All I'm askin'
Is for a little respect when you get home (just a little bit)
Hey baby (just a little bit) when you get home
(Just a little bit) mister (just a little bit)

I ain't gonna do you wrong while you're gone
Ain't gonna do you wrong 'cause I don't wanna
All I'm askin'
Is for a little respect when you come home (just a little bit)
Baby (just a little bit) when you get home (just a little

bit)
Yeah (just a little bit)

I'm about to give you all of my money
And all I'm askin' in return, honey
Is to give me my propers
When you get home (just a, just a, just a, just a)
Yeah, baby (just a, just a, just a, just a)
When you get home (just a little bit)
Yeah (just a little bit)

Chapter Thirteen – Florence Nightingale

Another strange, even spooky, anniversary occurred in the dreaded year of 2020. In May it marked the 200th Anniversary of the birth of the woman who created modern nursing, Florence Nightingale. How strange is that? Of all years eh?

I have a slightly obtuse connection with Florence as she lived in the Hampshire parish of Wellow and Sherfield English, as did I for many years, and her stately family home, Embley Park, became a school that both my daughters, Polly and Rosie, attended. Florence Nightingale was buried in the small village church of St Margaret's and it's in that tiny graveyard where our trip begins.

I have visited her grave many times to pay my respects, my history nut brain kicking in again, and each time I have gone alone and stood in silence. Today it is different because you are coming with me, to the church first of all and then to a museum in Chippenham which is shall explain shortly, but trust me it's something very special indeed, even though it may sound boring at the outset.

Finding the church is like looking for a needle in a haystack and so rather than meet you there, I'll take you there myself. It's off the A36, main link between Salisbury and Southampton but then it gets a bit more complicated. It's only a small church but it's steeped in so much Florence Nightingale history, so much so that you almost feel her presence.

As we walk into the church we see various postcards on sale related to her, but we turn right towards the alter. On our right hand side is a windowsill containing various pieces of original memorabilia including a cannonball from The Crimean War with a cross attached, made by a soldier in the battlefield hospital in Balaclava. There are haunting photographs of Florence in grubby frames, they have been there so long. We pay our respects and walk outside and directly in front of us, only about twenty feet away, is the grave with the simple inscription FN. Florence was offered a state funeral on her deathbed, together with a burial at Westminster Abbey but she declined, preferring to be laid to rest beside various members of her family and a return to Wellow where she spent so many years of her childhood. You stand beside me as we give thanks to the astonishing life of an astonishing woman.

We leave the church and make our way to Chippenham in Wiltshire, home of The Wiltshire Museum to view something quite remarkable.

Florence was an avid letter-writer, having written many thousand in her time, probably due to the fact she was bed-bound for many days of her life. I am working on a musical project relating to her and the rising of modern nursing and so we are given special access to the letters, a bit of VIP treatment. A metal vault the size of a large suitcase is placed before us on a table and its contents make our eyes pop from our heads. There they are, a selection of her letters, not copies, but the original letters. They make such interesting reading and they probably haven't been touched, some of them at least, for over a hundred years, and there they are, in a bundle tied with old string. There are envelopes, red, wax seals and numerous replies from other luminaries of the time, one of which we find incredible. It is an original letter sent to Florence by Isambard Kingdom Brunel, the man voted greatest Briton who has ever lived. We old the letter and delicately tough the ink. We tough Florence too and it gives us both goose pimples. It really is incredible history coming to life before our eyes, and we are carefully touching that history with our own fingers.

Neither of us have ever witnessed anything remotely like it before and we stand together as both Florence Nightingale and Isambard Kingdom Brunel, two of the greatest people ever to have lived, spring back to life just for me and just for you. How do you feel now? I had to write a tribute to the wonderful female pioneer;

N is for the nursing you gave to those in need
I is your monumental inspiration
G is for the gratitude of soldiers whom you saved
H is for your healthcare dedication
T is for the testament that stays with us today
I is how you fought intimidation
N is for the Notes on Nursing book you wrote
G is for our grateful generation
A is for the answer you gave to The Lord
L is for your social liberation
E is for the equal rights we fight for to this day

Florence Nightingale, our national salvation
I was born in Florence thus my name
The day of May 12th 1820
Into a world of privilege I came
Born into a family with plenty
I wanted for nothing
Absolutely nothing
Upper middle-class was my position
At the age of twenty-four
My mind made up for sure
With the help of God I came to my decision

I was never born to be a mother
I was never born to be a wife
Caring I considered as my lover
Caring I considered as my life

To be a wife and mother they had planned
That was where my wealthy life was going
I was born to offer more but they didn't understand
That my craving to care was ever-growing
The aristocracy
Didn't interest me
There was more to me than parasol and carriage
A peacock-feathered hat?
No I didn't fancy that
And neither did I think too much of marriage

I was never born to be a mother
I was never born to be a wife
Caring I considered as my lover
Caring I considered as my life

Social reform became my calling
My sights on equal rights were truly set
My father described it all as quite appalling
A passing phrase that I'd come to regret
No words would he hear
He turned the other ear
There was more to me than lunch in high places
Dear father if you knew
I don't want to live like you
So I'm not putting on yours airs and graces

My fight will not be over beyond the battlefield
That's when my fighting will begin
When the guns are silent and the flag of victory's raised
I will fight the fight few soldiers ever win
The scourge of the infantry
Pneumonia and dysentery
Hanging on to every single breath
My every bone is breaking
My every muscle aching
Please someone take me from these jaws of death

Battlefield angels came and rescued me
A frightened casualty of war

Battlefield angels came to hell and rescued me
They told me not to worry anymore
Through pestilence and pain
I never thought I'd walk again
But the battlefield angels came where no-one came before

I waved the white flag of surrender until I closed my eyes
I never thought I'd open them again
On the shoulder of a soldier I ended up in here
Hallucinating through such savage pain
Through damp foot and disease
Men dying to my left and to my right
Then a gentle word
In my ear was heard
Saying everything would be alright
Battlefield angels came and rescued me
A frightened casualty of war
Battlefield angels came to hell and rescued me
They told me not to worry anymore
Through pestilence and pain
I never thought I'd walk again
But the battlefield angels came where no-one came before

I signed and I sealed my letter of goodbye
Knowing I would never leave Ukraine
A casualty and a number nothing more than that
A soldier who would not see home again

As I feared the worse
Before my eyes appeared a nurse
Smiling as she gently mopped my brow
She never left my side
As I screamed in pain and cried
In my memory I still see her now

Battlefield angels came and rescued me
A frightened casualty of war
Battlefield angels came to hell and rescued me
They told me not to worry anymore
Through pestilence and pain
I never thought I'd walk again
But the battlefield angels came where no-one came before

    Yes, you came with me and touched her signature, the first to do so for over a century. A woman who did all that, her life's letters in a vault in Chippenham and together we touched them. How very, very special can a day be?

Chapter Fourteen – Brian May

Can you possibly imagine the thrill of playing a guitar duet with Brian May of Queen, one of the greatest guitarists in the world? In 1991 I did exactly that and it remains the greatest musical moment of my life. I couldn't believe Brian had agreed to appear on my TV show and even more surprised when he offered to do a song with me. I so wanted to meet him and assuming, you do to, I take you along to where it all happened.

I'm often asked who my favourite guitar players are and I have two, Brian May and Mark Knopfler. Many are surprised I never mention Eric Clapton and I understand that, but Brian and Mark both play electric guitars in an acoustic style, using their thumb and fingers and it's both difficult and beautiful. That's because they both started out playing fingerstyle on acoustic guitars.

It is to be filmed at The London Weekend Television studios on The South Bank just down from The Royal Festival Hall, now known as The London Studios.

We meet for rehearsals a few days before at The Pineapple rehearsal rooms just off Oxford Street, London. I have no idea how this rock icon's guitar-style will blend with my acoustic guitar, but I needn't worry because Brian has turned up with an acoustic guitar of his own. More than that, it is a cherished acoustic guitar his dad had made for him and he beams with pride as he takes it out of its case to show us, this musical piece of art. He is one of the friendliest guys you could ever wish to meet and our nerves soon disappear as he comes over and shakes our hands. He's very tall, as tall as a rock icon should be, and yet there is a certain softness about him.

We sat in the canteen and, over a cup of tea, as we work out the musical arrangement of the song we will perform on the show, with Brian proudly playing away on his dad's guitar.

It is truly wonderful to sit beside a world-famous musician who loves his music and more to the point got a real buzz out of playing that very special guitar. He is so proud of it and I feel chuffed when he invites me to have a play of it myself. The action on it is so good it plays itself. It is the start of event that neither you nor I will ever forget.

I'd sent him the song I wanted to do on a cassette a few days before, one of my new songs, called She's A Lady and he'd obviously put some work into it as he knows the song back to front as we sit down for our first run-through.

During a break for yet another cup of tea we came up with the idea of also using a string quartet to embellish the song and so it was that TV director John Kaye Cooper has booked four female classical musicians known as The Silver Strings and Brian helps to arrange the parts for them as I can't read music.

On the second day of rehearsal they turn up too and the sound of the two acoustic guitars along with two violins, viola and cello is enough to bring tears to a glass eye. I know the song well enough, so does Brian, but we keep running through it as I love the sound so much. I just can't get enough of it and I hope you are just as enthralled as myself.

It's now the evening of the filming and Brian begins with a beautiful guitar instrumental, Lost Horizon, from his new solo album. It is in true inimitable Brian May fashion, melodic and much bending of notes, played on his electric guitar. I've heard many times that Brian gets that unique sound of his by using a two-pence piece as opposed to a plectrum and to be honest I can't answer that as I didn't really notice. After much applause from the studio audience he then swaps guitars and joins me to film my song, She's A Lady, with The Silver Strings string quartet sat behind us in a semi-circle.

You sit in the audience to my right and I see the beaming smile on your face as the song rings out. You see how proud I am, although that probably isn't that difficult to see. We say our goodbyes to a wonderful man and musician, so pleased we both met such an incredible musician.

That performance is to this day a massive YouTube hit. It looked amazing and if I may be so arrogant it sounded amazing too. It all culminated in one of the proudest days of my life. Acoustic guitar or electric guitar, it didn't matter to me as I'd played with one of the world's greatest guitarists.

There is a well-kept secret to this story which I'd like to now expose because it confirms Brian May's extreme professionalism. We sang together on the very day that Freddie Mercury revealed to the press he had contracted AIDS and there were reporters swarming all around the TV studio trying to get at Brian for an interview. Brian ignored them all and just got on with the job in hand, a deed for which I'm eternally grateful. He must have been feeling dreadful at that particular time, but he never let it show for one moment. One can only wonder what he was going through and I give him full credit.

Planet Rock voted Brian May the 7th greatest rock guitarist of all time, yet I still remember him playing his dad's acoustic guitar at that rehearsal studio and picking away at the folkie 'If I Were A Carpenter.' In that same Planet Rock vote I never made the top ten million but I did once win the best guitarist in my road award. It didn't surprise me as I don't have any neighbours where I live. Oh, and I did play a guitar duet with the one and only Brian May and that's good enough for me. The 7th greatest rock guitarist of all time? Make that the first.

She looks in the mirror she mustn't be late
She's meeting him outside The Roxy at 8
She puts on her make up and zips up her jeans
She stays out much later now she's 17
She's a lady in everyone's eyes she's a lady

She hopes that her friends will see her tonight
But she'll feel like a queen on Monday alright

They'll ask what he tried and what she allowed
She'll say yes he tried he tried but he failed
She's a lady in everyone's eyes she's a lady

It's two in the morning they stand at her gate
He asks if she's happy oh yes it was great
Let's do it again on Saturday night
He kisses her neck and she whispers alright
She's a lady in everyone's eyes she's a lady

He gives her a light of her first cigarette
It's bad for her health but she tries to forget
She don't take it down but pretends that she did
Only yesterday she was only a kid
But she's a lady now in everyone's eyes she's a lady

She waits by the steps of The Roxy tonight
Perhaps he's been held up I hope he's alright
She waits til 8.30 and then through til 9
Her make-up is smudgy the end of the line
She's a lady in everyone's eyes she's a lady

She stops for a coffee and plays with the spoon
Perhaps there will be a new boy along soon
The tears fall away and a smile comes instead
I bet that he wasn't that stunning in bed
She's a lady in everyone's eyes she's a lady

Beautiful Brian May guitar solo

She looks in the mirror she mustn't be late
She's meeting him outside The Roxy at 8
She puts on her make up and zips up her jeans
She stays out much later now she's 17
She's a lady in everyone's eyes she's a lady

She hopes that her friends will see her tonight
But she'll feel like a queen on Monday alright
They'll ask what he tried and what she allowed
She'll say yes he tried he tried but he failed
She's a lady in everyone's eyes she's a lady

Chapter Fifteen – The Red Arrows

This magnificent team of pilots have helped me out on a couple of occasions when I've organised charity events. They flew over when I was raising funds for Lyme Regis Medical Centre and again when we started The New Forest Folk Festival. In more recent times I met up with them when I took part in The Great North Run. It makes you wonder if their pilots are super human. Fear not, they are just the same as us when they're not up in the sky, and to prove my point we're off to play golf with them.

The Reds, as we call them, have just returned from a training flight and rehearsal in Cyprus. Hang on! Rehearsal? In my game a rehearsal is when you get things wrong and keep going until you get it right. Surely there isn't much manoeuvre for getting it wrong when you're a Red Arrow? Anyway, I'm sure they know what they are doing.

As a matter of interest, the pilots spend six months from October to April practising for the display season. They wear green <u>flying suits</u> during training, and are only allowed to wear their red flying suits once they are awarded their Public Display Authority at the end of winter training and that's an important part of meeting them today.

The new pilots joining the team spend their first season flying at the front of the formation near the team leader. As their experience and proficiency improve, they move to positions further back in the formation in their second and third seasons. Pilots who start on the left of the formation stay on that side for the duration of their three-year tour; the pilots on the right side stay on the right. The exception to this are Reds 6 and 7, known as the Synchro Pair who fly in the 'stem' of the formation the two positions behind the team leader. Their concentration levels must be outrageous.

What may be of further interest is the pilots are called The Reds and the team that work behind the scenes, the mechanics etc, nearly a hundred of them, are called The Blues.

That's enough information. We're off to meet them at a charity golf event. They're based at RAF Scampton in Lincolnshire so we stay the night before at The Post House Hotel, as it was called back on this particular day up the top of the hill right next to Lincoln Cathedral. Let me tell you now, don't bother bring your alarm clock, the bells of the Cathedral will shake you out of bed quicker than you can say Rip Van Winkle.

It's a 9-hole course at a secret location and we arrive at 8.30am for the regulation coffee and bacon rolls before heading off to the practice green for a bit of putting practice. All golfers do that and I don't have the foggiest idea why. The putting green is nothing like the greens they are about to meet on the course. Hey, what do I know.

There are numerous celebrities dotted around, each doing their private bit for charity, including a team of footballers from Tottenham Hotspur, not my favourite team I have to admit, but I admire the fact they've turned out to play golf with us. The Red Arrows aren't too recognisable when they're not up in the air, but they have also provided a four-man team and we must be mixing with them during breakfast, we just don't know who they are.

The bell rings and the first team tee-off. You are quaking in your boots, full-knowing you're not the greatest golfer in Europe, and it's our turn soon.

Suddenly, four lads take to the first tee. They have got changed and they are all wearing pairs of red dungarees and they look magnificent, such a pleasant change from tartan trousers and stupidly patterned jumpers that golfers seem to wear as if it's some kind of a dare. It's the Red Arrows golf team and they look as fit as fleas.

Their first player places his ball down and everything falls silent. This ball is about to go into orbit. His swing looks good and the three-wood collides with the ball, sending it about twenty yards to the left, just missing one of the charity workers. The pilot falls to the ground with embarrassment and the rest of us fall to the ground in fits of laughter. So, you see, they aren't super human after all. It lightens the mood of the event and you aren't anywhere near as nervous as you were when you tee-off yourself. It's a day when you realise that not everyone is perfect and that has to go down as a point well proven.

As a respect thing I suppose, I wrote a poem in dedication to The Red Arrows and performed it on the

Channel Four television programme, Countdown, a little while later. It isn't a great poem as you may recall and I know you feel you can do better. You're probably right. In the meantime it's back to the noisiest alarm clock in the world before we heard for home.

Two wintry sparrows, each had a wintry cough
Sam and Sydney Sparrow bedraggled and cheesed off.
If only we were famous lamented Sam to Sid
Sam wanted to be famous he really really did

"We could fly in strict formation" said Sam in exultation
"We could be the famed Red Sparrows we will fly in strict formation
Shout it from the rooftops, tell your sisters and your brothers
Now let me see there's you there's me…. we need to find six others"

"We'll have all the things the Red Arrows have apart from jet propulsion"
Said the sparrows as they gathered in a tin of red emulsion
Eight Red Sparrows then soared high above the trees
And then in diamond shape they fell at 89 degrees

You could see they'd all been practising for the best part of six weeks
Cos' some had damaged feathers and the rest had buckled beaks

Now sparrows being sparrows, they had little skill as such
So no matter how they tried their displays weren't sadly up to much

Round and round the rooftops the Red Sparrows flew and flew
Under wing commander Sidney and Lieutenant Samuel too
Seven Red Sparrows…..yes, sadly one had gone
He'd swooped a bit too low and met a butcher's shop head on

They never had the smoke flares to leave a coloured trail
Except one who'd found a fag-end and strapped it to his tail
So no one knows exactly what occurred at Biggin Hill
The day the famed Red Sparrows had a catastrophic spill

Somersaulting, twisting, doing everything they'd learnt
Til they flew too close to a jumbo jet and were rather badly burnt
Some just lost some feathers some just got too hot
But Wing Commander Sydney I'm afraid he lost the lot

Two wintry sparrows, Sam and Sydney they are called
And Wing Commander Sydney is absolutely bald
Sitting in a forest tree protected from all weathers

And now you all know why poor Sydney's got no feathers
Two wintry sparrows, each had a wintry cough
Sam and Sydney Sparrow bedraggled and cheesed off.

Chapter Sixteen – Playing Cricket At Lords

Cricket isn't everyone's favourite cup of tea but I love the game and so I invite you to join me for a day at the sacred ground, Lords. To go to Lords is a wonderful experience, but to play there is another thing altogether. That's exactly what we are about to do. We take the tube to St John's Wood, a leafy, very middle-class area of London and walk to the ground, making a very special diversion as you may recall.

The ground is a reference to Thomas Lord who built the place, but it doesn't stand on its original site, it is the third of three grounds that Lord established between 1787 and 1814. His first ground was in Dorset Square and his second was used until 1813 when it had to make way for the building of Regents Canal, thus the term, being out for a duck. I have been invited to play by Sir David Frost, who is wicket-keeper because he can't run around too well.

We have lunch in The Long Room, a famous part of the ground where the tiny urn containing The Ashes is kept. It's lined, wall to wall, with paintings of famous cricketers going back to the 18th century. For contemporary or overseas players to have their portrait placed here is a considerable honour and very few have been awarded this distinction. For example, only four Australian cricketers have ever been honoured in this way, Sir Donald Bradman, Keith Miller, Victor Trumper and Shane Warne.

You enjoy your day at Lords but I just happen to know you enjoyed your walk to the ground even more, because I took you to Abbey Road, home of the most famous album sleeve of all time. That famous pedestrian crossing is at the southern end of Abbey Road, at the junction with Grove End Road and it is withing spitting distance of Lords Cricket Ground, not that cricketers spit as they tend to leave that to footballers.

Let's cross the road together shall we? You can be in front of me like John Lennon or at the back like George Harrison. We smile so much as we walk across that black and white piece of musical history. I love this experience so much, we both do, that I think it's worth adding some info I looked up;

The Beatles photo was taken on Friday, 8th August 1969 by Iain Macmillan. The police halted the traffic as he climbed up on a stepladder with his Hasselblad camera, you can imagine that happening today, not. The Beatles crossed the road three times and of course came back three times too. Of the six pictures taken Paul McCartney chose the fifth.

What I find most interesting is that the Beatles were working in different studios at the time. John, George and Ringo were recording I Want You whilst McCartney worked on Oh Darling elsewhere.

Anyway, it was a great day we shared together and I leave you to ponder if you preferred dining in The Long Room at the famous Lords Cricket Ground or crossing the road on the equally famous pedestrian crossing just down the road in Abbey Road. Much as I love my cricket I think I know which you are about to choose and I'm sorry Thomas Lord but I have to agree with you. So, barefoot or shoes on? Front like Lennon or back like Harrison? Let it be.

With regard to the origins of cricket
There are many conflicting tales
The sport began as some back garden fun
When the Tortoises challenged the Snails
An unlikely pair you'd think to yourself
Not being that fast or alert
But cricket's not a very fast game
And neither side could get hurt

Chapter Seventeen – Walking In Memphis

If you're a music nut like myself, then Downtown Memphis is a place you really must visit. It's all there, the history of music in one mind-blowing place. For instance, there's the famous Sun Studios where Elvis made his first recordings, where Roy Orbison was a session singer, plus so many other musical attractions. But there's somewhere else I want to take you, nothing to do with music, that will give you a lasting memory. We are about to travel off on a tangent.

We leave our hotel by the back entrance and walk across a kind of barren area towards Beale Street, made famous in Marc Cohn's song, Walking in Memphis. Yes, that's exactly what we're doing, we're walking in Memphis. It's a lengthy street of just under two miles, from East Street all the way down to the mighty River Mississippi. We pop into The Hard Rock Café on 315 Beale Street, the best Hard Rock Café in the whole world, before heading up the road, passing B.B.King's blues joint on our left. We could be going to Graceland to visit the grave of Elvis Presley, but I have other plans for us today, completely different plans to what you are expecting. You aske me where we are going and I tell you to wait and see.

At the top of Beale Street is a railway track that really does look like an old American railway track, hardly surprising as that's what it is, an old American railway track with rusty rails going across the road. We are making our way to the Lorraine Motel, at 450

Mulberry Street, just as Martin Luther King did on May 29th, 1968. It's time to stand where he was assassinated and pay our respects to the greatest civil rights activist of all time. A few days later, on April 4th, 1968 he was shot dead by James Earl Ray whilst standing on the upstairs balcony of Room 306.

When we arrive we are stunned by how small the motel actually is, probably because we both imagine Luther King making speeches to massive crowds. It wasn't the case at all. There's nothing spectacular about the building itself, it's tiny and looks a bit the worse for wear with its tired off-white walls and pale blue/green doors to the rooms. It looks more like a small hospital wing than a motel what with its tubular, bland balcony rails.

We stand on an incline opposite the inobtrusive building and realise it wouldn't have been too difficult to have heard him speaking without a microphone, he would have been that close to us. Just a few feet from where we stand history, a very sad history, was made and yet you would hardly think it as we stare up at Martin Luther King's room. I mention to you that it's so small he must have nearly hit his head on the roof above as he stood on that balcony.

We share a truly moving experience and words fail us. We return to the hotel exchanging very few words, it all being such a lasting impression. Beale Street is busy with music spouting out of every bar and coffee house, electric commercial blues and not the old blues the old boys used to sing back in the day, but it doesn't really seem to matter anymore. We think about going to Graceland to join the thousands of tourists and sight-seers but we choose not to as our trip to the Lorraine Motel was quiet and there were no such tourists milling around, just the two of us.

We all have dreams yet Martin Luther King had a far bigger dream than anyone could have imagined and for an hour of our lives we understood that dream and realised the dreadful consequences his dream caused. So many say it could have all been so different in America if he had lived, something we shall sadly never know, but I just had to bring you here.

Chapter Eighteen – Nelson Mandela

Whilst we are on the subject of political activists another great man springs to mind, Nelson Mandela. On a previous trip to America I had taken a boat for the short trip to Robben Island where he was imprisoned for 18 years, a true reality check and an experience to definitely share.

You would imagine from the set-up I'm taking you with me to Robben Island just off Cape Town and in full view to you when standing on the top of Table Mountain, but I went there on my own. I so want you to be with me and share the next part of my story.

We have flown to Sydney, Australia to join up with the P&O cruise ship Arcadia. The strange thing is we're joining the ship in Darwin, exactly 2,471 miles from Sydney and we probably flew over Darwin on our way down south. Ridiculous when you think about it.

A rather beautiful part of Sydney is known as The Rocks and we have checked in to The Holiday Inn on 55 George Street. It is mid-evening as we look out of our hotel window on quite a high floor and the mighty Sydney Harbour Bridge is to our left. We can't believe that people actually walk over the top of it, total madness in our opinion. Slightly hidden by the building opposite and across the harbour we see the Sydney Opera House which resembles an oyster painted by Andy Warhol. All is very pleasant what with the lights of the bars and restaurants below, but suddenly we see a sign, a billboard if you like, advertising an art exhibition by the one and only Nelson Mandela. Not many people know that Mandela was a brilliant artist and he produced many stunning artworks whilst imprisoned on Robben Island. He specialised in both pencil sketches and vibrant paintings of the brightest colours. Across the front wall is a large pink painting that bears the name freedom. Which kind of says it all.

Suddenly, something happens that both of us will remember for the rest of our lives. The great man himself, yes, Nelson Mandela, one of the most famous men in the world, appears from the building with a few photographers. Their bright lights illuminate the man and there he stands, before us, in all his splendour in a bright yellow tunic stroke kaftan. He has an aura around him to confirm his monumental importance. We can't believe our eyes and rush from the room to take the hotel lift down to the ground floor. He's standing there, with not too many people around, and we want to meet him. By the time we have crossed the road he has gone, there being no trace of him whatsoever. It is so weird. He's vanished into thin air and George Street is quietly going about its usual business. We were so near and yet so close.

To conclude this almost chance meeting that never quite happened, I told our story to a friend of mine, cricketer Robin Smith, who played for England but was born in Durban, South Africa. He knew Mandela quite well, having met him on a few occasions, and Robin gave me the Nelson Mandela autobiography signed by Nelson himself. It's very odd to think that

Nelson Mandela lived his life a million, trillion miles from mine and yet, through my trip to Robben Island off Cape Town , to that art exhibition in Sydney, Australia and finally that autobiography given to me in Southampton, I felt some kind of link with one of the greatest men ever to have lived.

      Nelson Mandela passed away on the 5th December, 2013, in Johannesburg but, as we both know, he will never die. Such an honour to have been so close and yet so many light years away, Mr Mandela.

Chapter Nineteen – Pinewood Studios

How would you like to join me on a conducted tour around one of the most famous film studios in the world? We're off to Pinewood, situated in the Buckinghamshire village of Iver Heath, 20 miles north of London. Make-up, lights and action.

We are off to a meeting with production company, One Media, at the invitation of Paul Shed, and they are situated right in the heart of the amazing place that oozes cinematic history. If I mention James Bond, Batman or the Carry-On films you will know what I mean. In more recent times they made Chitty Chitty Bang Bang, Bugsy Malone and outside shots for the Harry Potter movies were filmed in the woodland that surrounds the studios too. It's a truly monumental place.

Security is fierce, as you can imagine, and getting into the place could almost be a movie in itself. They lift the barrier and you think you're in, no chance. It takes nearly an hour for us to clear all the security checks but it's well worth the wait as we walk past the massive building where James Bond is filmed, and that's just the start of it. One Media are running late and so we have a chance to take a good look around. They kindly present us with an escort who knows the place inside out. It's the size of a small town so we need all the help we can get. But we start with a good old English cup of tea, as though we're in the company of Roger Moore. We leave the restaurant area through a Victorian conservatory behind us. But we are not talking any old conservatory as we just happen to be walking through the location for the splurge-gun fight of Bugsy Malone, starring Jodie Foster. Yet it all looks so tranquil as we recognise the various parts of the building from the film. Cream in your tea, sir? They could have asked couldn't they?

    Over a thousand cream pies were thrown around during that famous scene, using 1,000 gallons of synthetic cream in the process. Just look at it now, so serene and oh so very Victorian. You struggle to take it all in, we both do, as we are led out to the patio for a walk in the manicured gardens at the back of the building. Once again, we are not just talking any old garden, most certainly not. Don't forget, this is Pinewood Studios. We walk along a lawn towards a scene from Chitty Chitty Bang Bang, wondering as we go how Ian Fleming could possibly written James Bond and Chitty Chitty Bang Bang.

    The screenplay was written party by Roald Dahl and starred Dick Van Dyke and Sally Ann Howes and one of the joys of this 1968 film was that Dick Van Dyke didn't speak in that ridiculous cockney accent who adopted for Mary Poppins.

    There is a moment in the film when Sally Ann Howes, playing the part of Truly Scrumptious, a wealthy woman with a magical car, stands on an ornate bridge and sings Lovely Lonely Man. We stand on that very bridge. It's a beautiful design although the bridge doesn't doesn't actually go anywhere at the other end that isn't seen in the film. Apparently, the part of Truly

Scrumptious was first offered to Julie Andrews, to reunite her with Dick Van Dyke after Mary Poppins but she declined, saying the storylines were too similar.

Back indoors we take one last walk around the massive studio complex. Most have locked doors, not accessible to the public for obvious reasons, but we see the studio where they filmed part of Mamma Mia with Meryl Streep and Julie Walters. Again, we are blown away to be told the Greek house and some of the outside area was actually made of polystyrene. Oh well, never believe what you see in the movies.

Such a wonderful day and it was much better to share it with you than walk around these famous locations on my own. Fancy a splurge-gun fight?

There are many blue plaques at Pinewood, paying tribute to the many stars of comedy who filmed there back in the golden days of comedy, through all those Carry On films they made there. One, however is missing and he's my comedy hero, a great inspiration to me when, as a child, I listened to his weekly programme on the radio. The sadly-missed Tony Hancock, a comedy genius who never found himself that funny and someone who didn't actually live a fun-filled life. Never mind, I loved him and he made me laugh and so I pay my respects here;

Twinkle little star some stars will shine forever
Through classic songs like Elton John's on Marilyn Monroe
If I had the skill if I had the inspiration

There's one more twinkling star up there that wouldn't lose its glow

1924 was when the world first saw
A genius the likes of which they had never seen before
A television treasure who buckled with the pressure
But when we watch what's on these days we miss him all the more

In case you haven't guessed I'll give you his address
The Railway Cuttings 23 upon the door
Hancock was his name and only Tony Hancock
Could take just half an hour and make it last for evermore

He thought it was so harmful to give blood by the armful
Everyone remembers those immortal words he said
Hancock was the master of taking a disaster
And making it a story that would make you laugh instead

Like the Mayday call, neighbours banging on the wall
A message from a drowning man not getting through at all
No situation can rock a man like Tony Hancock
For he of 23 The Railway Cuttings life was cruel

Like the time he went away on two weeks holiday
Crates of milk and papers uncollected by the door

Hancock was his name and only Tony Hancock
Could take just half an hour and make it last for evermore

Deemed a wretched failure he flew off to Australia
Where East Cheam was to sadly seem a million miles from home
All those hours of pleasure and all those things we treasure
Despite it all they say Tony Hancock died alone

In 1968 on the 24th June
The final curtain closed on a genius too soon
And every time we say a pint of blood's an armful
That star up in the sky is shining brighter than the Moon

So I thought I'd write this rhyme to let you know the score
To tell you of a hero if you didn't know before
Hancock was his name and only Tony Hancock
Could take just half an hour and make it last for evermore
Yes Hancock was his name and only Tony Hancock
Could take just half an hour and make it last for evermore

Chapter Twenty – Ottery St Mary

Ottery St Mary is a small town in East Devon, ten miles east of Exeter. It's a beautiful part of the country but this town has a tradition that you are about to witness and I guarantee you will be frightened out of your skin. Dress up warm and make sure you wear a hat, don't say I didn't warn you. It has a population of around 5,000 but every 5th November you could almost put a nought on the end. It's heaving with crazy revellers who are continuing an age long tradition associated only with Ottery St Mary. Many are plied with alcohol and most are downright idiotic when it comes to personal health and safety.

So, let's just think about 5th November as it's a special date in the British calendar. It was the day dear old Guy Fawkes tried to blow up The Houses of Parliament and we celebrate that event. Ottery St Mary celebrate with a different kind of fire, very different bursts of flames. I reckon Guy Fawkes would find it all rather fun so it would have been nice to have invited him along too. Just don't let him near a box of matches;

It was in The Tower of London
Where Guy Fawkes lost his head
And that's not all he lost
Cos when it fell off he was dead

For trying to blow up Parliament
Guy Fawkes' head went flying

If he was here today
He'd get a knighthood just for trying

Guy Fawkes where are you?
Please come down from the sky
We know you failed the first time
Come and have another try

Some are left and some are right
They represent all classes
Guy Fawkes come and help us
They need rockets up their backsides

Guy Fawkes where are you?
I know you lost your head mate
But let me know even so
If you heard what I just said mate

I know you were a villain
I know you were a vandal
But can you come back down
And bring a ten ton Roman candle?

Don't bother bringing sparklers
Snowy storms or golden rain
Just bring the really noisy stuff
And sneak in there again

Guy Fawkes where are you?
If only Guy Fawkes was about

We need him more than they did before
To clear that nut-house out

Every year, for reasons way beyond anyone with any kind of sanity, tar barrels that have been set alight are carried through the streets of Ottery St Mary. It's an old custom said to have originated in the 17th century, and it's an annual event and we have been invited to carry such a barrel on our shoulders, something you would do best to decline. Each of the town's public houses sponsors a single barrel. In the weeks prior to the day of the event the barrels are soaked with tar and then lit outside each of the pubs in turn and once the flames begin to pour out the top and eventually the sides, they are hoisted up onto local people's backs and shoulders and they run through the town like those bulls in Spain.
The streets and alleys around the pubs are packed with people and seventeen barrels in all are lit over the course of the night as part of this traditional, very macho, event.
So here we are. In the afternoon and early evening there have been women's and boy's barrels racing on smaller shoulders, but as the evening progresses the barrels get larger and by midnight they weigh at least 30 kilos. A great sense of camaraderie exists between the 'Barrel Rollers', despite the fact that they tussle constantly for supremacy of the barrel. In most cases, generations of the same family carry the barrels with much pride.

Opinion differs as to the origin of this festival of fire, but the most widely accepted version is that it began as a pagan ritual that cleanses the streets of evil spirits. All we see is a bunch of nutters burning themselves with tar, as well as injuring many who are watching. Luckily, we are seated at a window above the local butcher's shop in the market square, thankfully safe from all harm with no intention of accepting their kind offer of us taking part.

Chapter Twenty-One – The Grand National

I've never been into horse-racing that much, but I have a dear friend who most certainly has. He's a great storyteller and you're coming to sit next to me around a table in the sleepy old town of Hunstanton in Norfolk.

I introduce you to Bob Champion, someone I've known for years and one of the bravest jockeys in the history of the sport.

Back in 1981 Bob won The Grand National at Aintree on board Aldaniti. What makes their victory so special is that they had both beaten serious illness, yes both jockey and horse, to be there in the first place, let alone win such a gruelling race.

Bob was diagnosed with testicular cancer in 1979, the very same cancer that killed my football hero, Bobby Moore, and Aldaniti suffered a serious leg injury that led to specialists saying he would never race again. He most certainly did race again and he lived another 17 years until he died of a heart-attack at the grand old age of 27. It's the kind of story that movies are made of and that's exactly what they did with the making of Champions in which Bob was played by John Hurt.

I did a few concerts for Bob when he founded The Bob Champion Cancer Trust and have enjoyed each other's company ever since.

We are at Le Strange Hotel in Hunstanton and Bob bounds in with an all too familiar grin on his face. He's lived through hell and come out the other side so he has every right to grin. The first thing you notice about him is that's quite stocky for a jockey, but I remind you many years and pints of beer have passed since the days when he rode racehorses. Quite short, yes indeed as all jockeys are, but broader than he used to be.

You are captivated when he tells about the most unlikely Grand National win in its history. Apparently Aldaniti nearly came a cropper at the first fence, catching it with his front leg, but the pair of them regathered their composure and went to win. There were 40 runners at the start but only 12 finished, with Bob and Aldaniti coming in 4 lengths ahead of the 8/1 favourite Spartan Missile. Bob in his usual understated manner will tell you it was nothing really and that, on the lovely sunny afternoon in Liverpool, he just happened to be on the right horse at the right time. It's all kind of humbling isn't it? A wonderful example of determination beating adversity.

Chapter Twenty-Two – Robin Williams

I think most of us agree that Robin Williams was one of the world's funniest performers before he left us under dreadful circumstances on 11th August, 2014. Who could ever forget Good Morning Vietnam? We all know there is often tragedy behind comedy, it's quite a formidable list; Tony Hancock, Tommy Cooper, Jim Carrey, Lenny Bruce, Richard Pryor and John Belushi.

I'm about to play The London Palladium with him for The Prince's Trust and, as he has the dressing room next to mine, I thought you'd like to say hello.

He is leaning against the wall in the backstage corridor between the two dressing rooms, wearing a green, baggy sweater, a kind of fisherman's smock, and the first things you notice are his enigmatic smile and his height. He's far shorter than you could ever possibly imagine. He shakes our hands with a level of courtesy, a soft handshake that gives away an element of shyness and uncertainty. He's one of those entertainers who simply explodes like a stick of dynamite when he gets up on stage or in front of a camera, but right now he's fairly relaxed.

Normally, when you work in front of The Royal Family, as was the case here, your material is vetted to ensure its suitability, but Robin Williams tells us he's having none of that. He has been booked as Robin Williams and Robin Williams he will be.

During my own rehearsal you stand beside him on the side of the most famous stage in the world. He nods and smiles at my 200 Remembers routine, no fits of laughter I hasten to add, and he tells me what a great subject matter days gone by is.

Come the evening performance Prince Charles and Princess Diana enter the Royal Box and I start the show. Elton John, a favourite of the Princess, bashes out a few songs and then this firework explodes onto the stage with an energy I've never seen before. Of course, as was stated later, we now know why, but we both marvel at his stagecraft.

After the show there are drinks with the Royals at a special location but there is no sign of the comedy genius. He has disappeared into the night, but at least we met him and shook his hand.

Chapter Twenty-Three – Theatre Royal, Windsor

This is a very short recall and visit with you because I have no intention of being disrespectful of The Royal Family, but of course The Theatre Royal is their local theatre when they are in residence at the castle. It's a tiny theatre compared to most, wedged between various buildings in Thames Street with only just enough space to breath. In fact, it's so cramped there is only one side of stage area as the other is a brick wall. It doesn't even have a car-parking area so I have no idea how the bigger shows load in their gear and stage scenery. I'm sure they have a way though.

I take you onto the raked stage and the seats seem to rise upwards as far as they go back. To our right we look up and see probably the smallest Royal Box anywhere in any theatre. It is a box with a difference though because it has its very own toilet. I suppose it's nothing unusual when you think about it as you'll never see The Queen or any other member of The Royal Family queuing up with the punters, and yet it strikes me and you as very funny.

The soundcheck is complete and the stage crew have gone off for their dinner, leaving us alone in the theatre with some time to kill. Yes of course I know we shouldn't, but it has to be done. We leave it to everyone else to wonder exactly what we got up to but we acted like naughty schoolchildren, messing around behind the teacher's back. That's all we need to tell anyone on the subject but let's just say the stage crew nipping off for their dinner made things rather convenient.

It isn't one of my proudest moments of my adult life but oh how we laughed all the way home.

Chapter Twenty-Four – Lincoln Theatre Royal

Whilst we are on the subject of Theatre Royals you must come with me to The Theatre Royal, Lincoln and share another truly amazing moment and story. I have already recalled the time we visited The Mohne Dam in Germany, scene of The Dambusters attack, but there is a parallel here as The Theatre Royal, Lincoln is the nearest theatre to their base at RAF Scampton.

It has its own place in theatrical history. Firstly, Jeffrey Archer, the famous author, worked there is 2002 as a stage-hand whilst serving a jail sentence for perjury at the nearby North Sea Camp Prison. Backstage at this theatre is quite something else isn't it? The theatre was built in 1893, long before they had to worry about car-parking quite obviously and as you enter the tiny stage door in a side street you turn right to go into the theatre itself or left to reach the dressing rooms. There is actually a kind of wooden bridge joining the two and it's so cute and even enchanting.

Far more interesting than Jeffrey Archer is the fact that Guy Gibson, squadron leader of the 617 Dambuster Squadron, sat up in the circle gallery and looked down at the stage. As he did so he noticed the two spotlights on the left and right hand side of the stage converge in the middle where the entertainer stood at the time. It was a Eureka moment for Gibson who had been wondering how The Lancaster bombers could fly at the correct height as they approached the dam, and there was the answer, before his very eyes in

The Theatre Royal, Lincoln. Barnes Wallis's bouncing bombs had to be dropped at a critical height or they either sank or exploded too quickly and Gibson found the answer here and left at the interval, hot-footing down to Bomber Harris in The War Office in London.

Just like time at the Windsor equivalent we are standing on the stage looking out at the empty seats during my soundcheck when a stage crew member tells us that amazing story and so, once again, it has to be done. After soundcheck we climb the narrow stairs, narrow but covered in rich, red carpet and we both take our place in the circle gallery where Guy Gibson sat on that night. It's a spine-chilling moment for us both.

Chapter Twenty-Five – The Bottom Line

It's 1975 and we're flying down to New York as I'm playing at The Bottom Line. That may not sound too spectacular but just hang on a moment. It was a 400 seater venue in Manhattan, on 15 West 4th Street, wedged between Mercer Street and Greene Street and for a few years it was the place to play in New York. Its owner, Alan Pepper, invited me to play there as a support to folky singer/songwriter Tom Rush.

I have never suffered from any nerves or stage fright but if it was ever going to happen it would be here. It had only been open a couple of years when we went there but Bruce Springsteen and Lou Reed had already played a few gigs there along with so many others, creating a list as long as your arm. I will try not to bore you but when you see the kind of performer that had played there, at that small place, then you will understand why it was so very special.

They had a kind of rule there that everyone who played there had to touch the grubby white wall above the tiny door that led to the stage once three rickety steps had been negotiated. Not only did the wall have to be touched but it had to be signed too.

We both stand in wonder as we check out the numerous signatures. There were so many 'oh my god's' as we suddenly notice yet another star name. To list them all would take forever but here are some names on that wall that led out to the tiny auditorium;

Eric Clapton, Springsteen and Lou Reed of course, Dolly Parton, Prince, Carl Perkins, Sting, Barry Manilow, and two names that surprise us both, Peter Cook and Dudley Moore.

Shortly before my appearance there Peter Cook and Dudley Moore had recorded a very rude album called Derek and Clive, an album of filth but very funny just the same. As politically incorrect as it could be in these modern times, but quite acceptable back in the day.

Just when we think we've seen them all, you nudge me and there are more signatures where you are standing;

Dire Straits, Van Morrison, Daryl Hall and John Oates, Linda Ronstadt, Bryan Ferry, blues and folk legend Doc Watson, Emmylou Harris and Indian sitar supremo Ravi Shankar. We tell me to sign the wall too and I duly oblige. You never know, someone one day may well recognise my signature, as if.

In these modern times it would have made for a brilliant photo on your mobile phone, but such things didn't exist back then.

Remember a world without mobile phones?
Days before ear-splitting ringing tones?
When people could shop without making a call?
When kids played games on the way home from school?
Scrumping for apples and running for our lives
Before society allowed kids to have knives
A clip round the ear from the local copper

These days he would come a cropper
Where is it going? I've no idea
Where is it taking us? Can anyone hear?
Through rhymes we can shout about it
But who will do anything about it?

    The gig went ok, although I admit I never set the world on fire and we made our way back to the St Moritz Hotel at 50 Central Park South, overlooking, obviously, Central Park, very close to where John Lennon was assassinated a few years later.

    It has been quite some evening and we sit down to enjoy a beer in the bar overlooking the park. All is peaceful until I notice one of my heroes sitting at a table adjacent to ours, blues guitarist Rory Gallagher. We just have to go over and say hello to this shy Irishman. He is so friendly and our short chat with him closes an eventful evening so far from home. We both agree that if we could have taken home any of those signatures and stuck them on our wall, then we would have forsaken them all for that of Rory Gallagher.

    Four years later Rory appeared on my Capital Radio show in London and he actually remembered meeting me at The St Moritz that night. Rory Gallagher died on 14th June, 1995 at the age of 47, and a lump comes into my throat as I conclude this time him, you and I sat and enjoyed a beer together.

    The Bottom Line opened and closed a few times as it struggled to survive with Bruce Springsteen even offering to pay the back-rent it owed. That incredible gesture on its own confirms what an important venue The Bottom Line was. Harry Chapin did his 2,000th gig there in later years and Joan Baez played there too in 1995, along with Janis Ian, Richard Thompson and Suzanne Vega and that's why still it remains a bastion of wonderful music and memories.

The Bottom Line is that it opened its doors on February 11th 1974 and gave so many performers their first chances of making a name for themselves. Another trip you wouldn't have missed for the world?

Chapter Twenty-Six – The City Varieties

Now then, if you think The Bottom Line in New York was steeped in history then you must compare it with The City Varieties in Leeds. Now I really am taking you back to the days of British Music Hall. Many years ago they filmed a TV show called 'The Good Old Days' from this beautiful monument of music and I played more times than I care to remember. Before I take you there and lead you round the meandering staircases backstage please allow me to tell you about the place because we are visiting a theatre that saw performances by Charlie Chaplin, Max Miller and Houdini, along with literally thousands of others.

This theatre was built in Swan Street in 1865, long before Leeds had one-way systems that made it difficult to even find the place, let alone perform there. Yes, it's a true Victorian Music Hall. The theatre is long and very thin, indeed so thin you can stand on stage and almost touch the two balcony boxes either side of you.

You are joining me for my last performance there on 11th and 12th October 2002. You are bemused by the poster outside, as indeed am I. It reads as follows;

Richard Digance, Renowned Raconteur – Steve Barclay, The Furtive Funster – Jane Webster the Delightful Diva – Delia Du Sol, Contrived Convolutions and Joan Hinde, Britain's Foremost Female Trumpet Player. Oh yes, they don't produce posters like that anymore.

The passing years haven't really changed the backstage area too much and being behind the curtains is just as interesting as the theatre itself. The main dressing-room is just big enough to have a sink and a mirror and its door takes us to a seating area, a kind of green room, between us and the stage. The dodgy stone steps lead us up to stage level, they being so narrow it's difficult not to crash into the sides or bang your head on the rafters of the stage. Up another flight of undisciplined stairs leads us a backstage area the same level as the balcony boxes. The walk across the gangway beside the old stage lights leads us to the auditorium itself. We walk along the side of the upper floor until we reach the old bar at the back, a very special bar at that. It contains signed phots and programmes in glass cabinets to protect them from the elements. Some pictures are over 100 years old and they show the theatre in all its glory.

I had to bring you here so you could see, taste and smell the old days of entertainment that have now sadly disappeared.

For that appearance in 2002 and I was asked to write a song in the tradition of old cockney music hall;

Here's a sympathetic song about a Mr Sydney Strong
Who became an institution in the place where I belong
He worked throughout the night coming home when it was light
I shouldn't really tell ya cos it really wasn't right
But Mr Sydney Strong he was a tealeaf

Which means in cockney rhyme he was a criminal
He even nicked the fillings from his granny's teeth
And if Grandad was alive he'd nick from him an all
But now he's locked away, he was sentenced yesterday
But if you was with him now let me tell you what he'd say

Don't come round for me tonight Bill
I'm otherwise detained tonight am I Bill
Tonight I'm all alone so you'll be drinking on your own
Don't come round for me tonight Bill

Now Mr Sydney Strong had a Mrs call Yvonne
They say she fell off the back of a lorry and I doubt if they were wrong
She's a good one Sid you should get married so he did
He nicked the marriage licence cos he hadn't got a quid
Everybody loved Yvonne and Sydney, Everybody said he could do worse
The finest pair around since steak and kidney
The finest pair since Peters and Geoff Hurst
But the wedding ring he got was unquestionably hot
It made her finger smoulder like a dumpling in a pot
So when the copper got his scent off the Pentonville he went
And to his best mate Billy this little note was sent

Don't come round for me tonight Bill
I'm otherwise detained tonight am I Bill
Tonight I'm all alone so you'll be drinking on your own

Don't come round for me tonight Bill

Now such a clever thief was he, He nicked the prison key
So after dark to Upton Park he nipped off for his tea
He and dear Yvonne kissed and cuddled all night long
Before the dawn was breaking he made sure that he was gone
Such a devil, naughty devil was our Sydney
He broke into a pub and a tobacconist
Sydney had more front than Harrods didn't he
Every night he smoked and got extremely ... drunk
Although he's stuck inside he leaves a message every day
He leaves it for the coppers every time he runs away

Don't come round for me tonight Old Bill
I'm otherwise detained tonight am I Old Bill
Tonight I'm all alone so you'll be drinking on your own
Don't come round for me tonight Old Bill

Don't come round for me tonight Bill
I'm otherwise detained tonight am I Bill
Tonight I'm all alone so you'll be drinking on your own
Don't come round for me tonight Bill

The days of British Music Hall are sadly long in the past now, something we are reminded of when the master of the music hall, Roy Hudd, passed away in 2020. Roy would have hated to have seen so many theatres close their doors later in the year, it would have broken his heart. I last worked with Roy at The British Music Hall Society gathering in Eastbourne in 2019 and I'm sure you remember how full of beans he was as we shared a cup of tea in my dressing room. He lived for the theatre but, like those theatres, he never made it through the worst year of our lives. No encores but a brilliant life well-lived, sir.

Chapter Twenty-Seven – Worthing

My good friend, Mike Payne, has invited you to join us at an Italian restaurant after my show at Worthing Pavilion. He has something very special to show us. It's just across the road from the theatre and we go down the steps into a posh cellar with tables adorned in red tablecloths, an important part of the story. It's a beautiful summer's evening in August 1985.

Mike is a cartoonist who worked as a tax inspector at The Inland Revenue until I rescued him from such a painful and thankless existence by having him appear on my television show. We created a spoof weather forecast with Mike supplying drawings of The Cloud Crowd. He is now a full-time cartoonist and animator working for Carte Blanch Greetings Cards based in Sussex.

We enjoy a lovely Italian meal and Mike is excited to tell us both about a wonderful little character he has just created and he is wondering what we both think of it. He takes a felt-tip pen from the inside-pocket of his jacket, Mike always wears a jacket regardless of the heat, and he proceeds to draw his new character. It's a brilliant concept, a little animal, and he has even come up with a name for it, Tatty Teddy.

You have just attended the world premier of the biggest selling bear in the world that has grossed over two billion pounds in its time.

Tatty Teddy? Yes, he has just drawn, on a red napkin at our table, the little grey bear, covered in stitches with the sky-blue nose. It would only be a matter of time before this little drawing would end up on literally millions of greetings cards, key-rings, mugs, coasters and tags. You name it and Tatty Teddy will be there. It will become a figurehead product for Clintons Cards as time passes and there he is, sitting there on the red tablecloth in that Italian restaurant. Mike and I go on to produce various greeting cards for Carte Blanch but none are ever as popular as Tatty Teddy. I should the little creature really, but he's adorable. You agree and so does Mike's bank manager.

If only you had walked out of the place clutching that little masterpiece he drew on that napkin. It would be worth a fortune. And it all began with The Cloud Crowd;

Clouds are truly amazing things
like white balloons in the sky without strings.
They move to the left or to the right.
Some even disappear from sight.

Where do they go? that's a surprise
when they disappear before your eyes
Now you are about to find out
what their lives are all about.

The Cloud Crowd live above your head
when you're awake or in your bed.
Some are white and some are grey
and they're above you every day.

Here they are each and every one,
here to let you share their fun.
They only stay a little while,
just long enough to make you smile

Chapter Twenty-Eight – Film Extras

Hey we nearly made it to the silver screen didn't we? I have possibly been likened to George Clooney or Tom Hanks, or maybe I haven't, I can't remember now, but it was a close-run thing in 1975 when I'd gone walkabouts in Central City and Silver City, Colorado. I was signed to Mercury Records in The United States and they sent me all over the place to publicise the release of my album over there. I would love to have shared what happened in the next few hours but I never did, until now. You should have been there and now you are.

I seemed to be in the middle of nowhere when I stumbled across the most ridiculous wooden sign beside a bolder about half the size of a car. The sign stated that I was looking at the highest rock in the Rocky Mountains range. Oh really! How could they possibly know? The Rocky Mountains were formed over 60 million years ago and this little bolder didn't look old enough to have started nursery school. Something didn't quite add up. Now then, the Rocky Mountains stretch 3,000 miles from Canada down to the Rio Grande in New Mexico and I don't have the foggiest idea how high they are. I very much doubt if most Americans don't have any idea how high they are either. But the Americans love producing tourist attractions in their history-steeped country and my trip to Colorado confirmed that. This state claims that various western legends holed out there, including Butch Cassidy, Wyatt Earp, Buffalo Bill and Doc Halliday, So it was no surprise to me that my solitary magical mystery tour landed in a place that resembled an old cowboy town.

My observations were correct but not in the way you imagine. My mystery trip has ended up on a working film set and we both want to see more of what's going on. Neither of us have ever been near a film set in our lives and so it's all very interesting.

They are filming a scene for the 1976 movie The Duchess and the Dirtwater Fox with George Segal in the role of The Dirtwater Fox and Goldie Hawn as The Duchess. I don't think it will go down in history as a blockbuster of gigantic proportions but maybe it would have done better at the box office if we'd both been in it. The strange thing is we nearly were, as you about to recall. What is the film about? I've no idea but there's a stagecoach parked next to our hire-car and various people walking around in costume so my hunch is it's going to be yet another western.

Looking like some down and out folkie, which wasn't too far from the truth in 1976, some lady with a clip board assumes I'm not a tourist at all, but an extra waiting to be told where to plonk myself in front of the camera. I am totally confused and I can only imagine you are too.

As I say, I know very little about this film, even film-buff friends of mine have never heard of it but if that lady with the clip-board hadn't ask to see my union card I could have been in the opening bar-room, bawdy scene and you would have been there too. Just imagine how the box-office had gone through the roof if we'd been in it.

I was gobsmacked how many people were working behind the scenes. They all looked so important as they scampered around like little black ants clutching scripts and stopwatches. They were everywhere, but it was time to move on. We thought about measuring the height of that bolder but we couldn't be bothered.

Chapter Twenty-Nine – Whitechapel Road

I'm off to London and I wonder if you'd like to join me? I'm visiting a special shop and we're not talking Harrods or Selfridges. I'm off to the other end of London, to the district of Whitechapel. I've made this pilgrimage twice before but both times I was on my own. This time I fancy sharing the emotion.

We all know Whitechapel is synonymous with The Kray Twins, but they are not my subject matter. We travel down the Whitechapel Road, further into the city than The Blind Beggar pub that was frequented by Reggie and Ronnie. I have no real interest in Jack The Ripper either.

All I want to do is stand outside 259, Whitechapel Road and soak up the history, indeed history that sends shivers down my spine. It's difficult to walk along that side of the road due to the multitude of market stalls, it's busy in the extreme. In fact it's so busy it's easy to walk straight past 259 Whitechapel Road, a small shop that sells Indian Saris. Opposite the shop is The London Hospital and that is the connection because No 259 was where they exhibited Joseph Merrick, the Elephant Man, like some circus freak. Some laughed and some broke down in tears as he sat in the shop window like some monkey in a cage and I first went and stood there about 20 years ago, maybe more, to personally apologise to his memory for how humanity had treated him.

We will stand there together and very few people, if any, will know the reason why we are standing there in silence, deep in thought and respect.

His deformed skeleton is apparently stored in The London Hospital. The museum behind displays Merrick's twisted torso but it is a Plaster of Paris replica. That's the spooky thing about our service. We can stand and look across the road to The London Hospital and somehow engage with what the poor man went through. I suppose it's an elongated three-minute silence.

Joseph Carey Merrick was born in the year of 1862 and he died in The Royal London Hospital in 1890 age of just 27 years

In the words of the man himself;

I first saw the light on the 5th August 1862 when I was born in Lee Street, off Wharf Street, in Leicester. The deformity which I am now exhibiting was caused by my mother being frightened by an elephant

Victorian East London, with its dark and dingy back streets, was a hard place to survive. It was a time of poverty and disease and at that time it was laced with accusations regarding the identity of street murderer Jack The Ripper.

Even Joseph Merrick himself had the finger pointed at him. The Bobbies, the London police, were out in force but never once did they protect the safety and the well-being of The Elephant Man.

They were far more interested in stealing the pocket-watches of drunkards rolling in the street, thus the term 'if you want to know the time ask a policeman.'

Joseph Carey Merrick by name
If not fortune would soon find fame
People travelled for miles it is said
To see the man with the elephant head
They gasped and laughed at him
But he took it all on the chin
Sat like a doll in his brand new abode
In a shop window in Whitechapel Road
Sat like a doll in his brand new abode
In a shop window in Whitechapel Road

He never smiled as onlookers came
He sat like a photo without any frame
Even royalty visited him
knowing his heart was broken within
Nobody cared about that
As they gathered where Merrick sat
Not knowing his heart was about to explode
In a shop window in Whitechapel Road
Not knowing his heart was about to explode
In a shop window in Whitechapel Road

There he sat like a bear in a cage
In the shop that became his theatrical stage
Tears were unashamedly shed
As Joseph repositioned his head

Through the man with elephant skin
Tom Norman was coining it in
There he sat like a tormented toad
In a shop window in Whitechapel Road
There he sat like a tormented toad
In a shop window in Whitechapel Road

Oh my god some people would say
But even so their eyes wouldn't stray
Hoping for a wave or maybe a smile
That's why they travelled for many a mile
Come and see if you can
The incredible elephant man
Skin like leather a nose like a trunk
Sitting there just like a demented drunk
Skin like leather a nose like a trunk
Sitting there just like a demented drunk

Doctor Treves saved the day
When the London surgeon took him away
Joseph Merrick came to be
A friend of the aristocracy
At high places he was seen
He had an audience with the Queen
By the fact that he was badly abused
Queen Victoria wasn't amused
By the fact that he was badly abused
Queen Victoria wasn't amused

It's hard to believe that people treated other people is such a dreadful, shameless manner. But that's exactly what they did and we've turned up today to say we are sorry.

Chapter Thirty – Mickey

My final story is something that happened just a few years ago, far more recent than some of the events I have mentioned and re-lived with you by my side.

I was patron of a charity, Dave Lee's Happy Holidays, based in Kent and run by one of my very best friends. Dave died just a few years ago and so it was time to close the charity down and use the funds still in the bank to take 53 under-privileged kids to EuroDisney in Paris. Imagine the delightful chaos. I really could have done with you by my side. Yes, you really should have been there.

I hate theme parks and the frightening attractions you are supposed to enjoy, so it would have helped me if you'd gone up The Tower of Terror instead of me. I did it though, with gritted teeth.

The highlight for the wide-eyed children was having breakfast with the one and only Mickey Mouse, a creature who was much bigger than I expected. I've always thought of mice as being little things that run around the kitchen if you leave the kitchen door open, certainly not the size of this one.

The kids were all excited as they took their places in the place where he would appear. Some were in wheelchairs, obviously, and so I needed to mark Mickey's card, to make sure he would stumble into them with his limited vision, if you see what I mean. So, I waited outside while the kids tucked into their grub and fizzy drinks until the most famous mouse in the whole world turned up, which he did. It's a fantastic set-up at EuroDisney, really fantastic. I know very little about the logistics, how they make it all work, because you never see any of the characters strolling around. They just turn up at a given time, all very clever. Perhaps there is a maze of underground tunnels, I have no idea. Anyway, Mickey arrives and he's standing behind a wall, waiting to appear and I catch him before goes in. He's leaning against a wall as I explain about the wheelchairs included in my party of kids and he nods and says with an American accent 'Cool, man, I get it.'

With that he enters the restaurant and waves, pats the kids on the head and poses for numerous photographs. He walks down the aisle and crashes straight into a wheelchair. 'Cool,man, perhaps you didn't get it after all.' I couldn't quite see but I think he looked me in the eyes with immense embarrassment as I straightened his spotted bow-tie. Luckily for all he didn't lose his head in more ways than one. He kept his demure persona and carried on with the job in hand bring so much pleasure to my little warriors. Credit where it is due I have to admit. It was like me breaking a guitar string on stage, the show always goes on.

Yes, you should have been there, as should my best mate Dave Lee have been too. So many smiles on so many little faces and a huge smirky grin on yours too if you'd seen the mouse go flying. In all fairness though, Mickey Mouse is getting on for 100 years of age so he's done well to turn up on time. No memory loss because he turned up and lots of stamina that I envy at my age, and I'm much younger than that, despite the rumours.

My trip to Paris with the 53 kids inspired me to write about Mickey. Was he first cartoon character to appear in Great Britain? Many will guess he was but I'm not so sure.

You were the first
 the quickest on the draw
You were the first,
Yes you were the first
none had gone before
You were the first
Yes you were the first

It's a question often asked
who was the first they drew
Some will tell you it was Mickey Mouse
but it wasn't it was you
It was 1928 when Steamboat Willie came ashore
Enter Mickey Mouse
but you came eight years before

You were the first
 the quickest on the draw
You were the first,
Yes you were the first
none had gone before
You were the first

Yes you were the first

If it wasn't Mickey Mouse
it was Felix some will say
Those who tell you TinTin
are another year away
1929 Popeye's boat they steered
It took another three years
before Superman appeared

You were the first
 the quickest on the draw
You were the first
Yes you were the first
none had gone before
You were the first
Yes you were the first

So who Is the oldest
who's been around the longest
In a crazy cartoon world
who's proved to be the strongest
It wasn't Donald Duck
Batman or Bugs Bunny
If you're betting on the oldest
then Rupert takes the money

You were the first
 the quickest on the draw
You were the first,

Yes you were the first
none had gone before
You were the first
Yes you were the first

They followed in your footsteps
where none had gone before
You were the first
You were the quickest on the draw

You were the first
 the quickest on the draw
You were the first,
Yes you were the first
none had gone before
You were the first
Yes you were the first

The Little Things In Life

The little things I can no longer touch
A gentle hug and kiss yes that is what I miss
I can't believe my life and times are playing out like this
As my days grow ever dark and long
I can't believe such little things have gone

Shaking hands is something of the past
Shaking heads now, how long will this last?
Just an empty room to emphasise such gloom
I have no-one to talk to other than the Moon
I hope my new friend sees me through the night
At the end of this dark tunnel it's my light

Respite I seek with each new day
A return to where the little children play
Where people laugh and sing and Sunday church-bells ring
The smiles on the faces that conversations bring
I wonder is this all too much to ask?
Is my smile forever hidden by a mask?

It's the little things we have to keep alive
The little things in life that must survive
The bustling arcade the celebratory parade
Students in the lecture hall trying to make the grade
In this time of darkness and despair
Words seem to be the one thing we can share

It's made me realise that words are strong
They help us all to right things that are wrong
The time is to believe that words will never leave
Words are always here to send or to receive
Words are always here to keep us strong
When all the little things in life have gone

There's the places you have been to
The faces you have seen
So many days you spent with me
So many years in between
But you were there beside me
On every special day
And the beauty of it all is
Memories never pass away

It's possibly the aftershock of 2020 and all it brought us that made me think back on the days when I wandered around as free as a bird, when we were all allowed to do such a thing, taking in so many places and meeting so many new faces. It all seems so long ago now doesn't it? Yes, it is sad that sometimes you do so many great things and see so many great places when you are on your own and cannot share such moments, but these pages have allowed me to return to such days with you by my side. The book title says you should have been there, yet in a strange way you were there, albeit second time around. You came along at my invitation and you shared some moments that I have kept to myself over the years, with the odd exception that I've enjoyed bragging about at dinner parties.

I began the book by defining loneliness. I wasn't at all lonely on any of these days but, even so, I would loved to have not been on my own because I would have had the proof that these great days actually happened. So, thank you for your company.

ACKNOWLEDGEMENTS

It is both customary and correct to acknowledge those mentioned in any book and I therefore do so with my thanks to those I list below.

In some way or other the people here have affected my working life directly or indirectly. All those mentioned below I knew personally, obviously some more than others which goes without saying, and they all induced great memories that I have had a chance to share with you by my imaginary side. Every event mentioned I undertook on my own but I am delighted to be doing exactly the same again with someone to share each moment, each very special moment of my life.

You certainly don't have to trawl through such a long list of names below if you don't fancy the challenge as you've already read all about them in previous pages, but as I say it's the right and proper thing to do, to acknowledge anyone you mention in a book and so I am delighted to do so with gratitude to them. Some have sadly passed away now and I think of them dearly. They may be gone but they are certainly not forgotten.

Having said all that, if you do wish to trawl through them all, have a browse at your leisure and see how many stories you can recall. I suppose it's a bit like a pub quiz without the pub. It is written at a time there are no pub quizzes and fewer pubs and so they are memory in themselves. None of us will have great memories of 2020 and so I went further back and dug deeper to cheer myself up. I hope some of these stories have cheered you up too, because if that is the case my job is done and I feel satisfied. Old age brings a loss of memory, and of course despair and brute loneliness, but my brain will never allow it to happen to me, I certainly hope not anyway. We never know what's around the corner, of course we don't, but I just thought it would be good to pass on such wonderful memories whilst I wallow in such nostalgia.

In the meantime I will leave you with a more recent memory, of times before The Third World War when I used to stand in front of an audience and sing my songs and tell my stories. Blimey that seems a long time ago right now doesn't it? But on the upside, I had the time to recall so many amazing days of my life.

We are together for the evening, together me and you
Cos that's what performers and audiences do
Isn't it peculiar that your day's nearly done
Me i'm quite the opposite, mine has just begun
Yet here we are together to share an hour or two
Cos that's what performers and audiences do

You look at me and I look at you
Cos that's what performers and audiences do
We watch from here and you all sit down there
Judging if our skills are in a state of disrepair
Some of you will clap and some of you will boo
Cos that's what performers and audiences do

Up here we do one man shows, musicals or plays
Then performers and audiences go their separate ways
We get on the road again after every show
Cos after each performance that's where performers go
Motorways at midnight through the dark to somewhere new
Cos after each performance that's what performers do

With the truckers and the traders the motorways are ours
It's all part of the job driving through the early hours
Coffee at the services home at half past two
After each performance that's what performers do
That all happens later, right now it's me and you
Cos that's what performers and audiences do

      I hope the list makes you smile as they help you recall the stories you've read in this book. Good Luck.

- Elkie Brooks
- Marc Cohn
- Sandy Denny
- Leonard Digance
- Kenny Everett
- Gerald Ford
- Sir David Frost
- Rory Gallagher
- Gordon Giltrap
- Rod Hamilton
- Steve Hewlett
- Roy Hudd
- Alan Hull
- Elton John
- Trevor Jordan
- Nat Joseph
- Nic Kinsey
- Sonja Kristina
- Dave Lee
- Mike Oldfield
- Sally Oldfield
- Steve Martin
- Brian May
- Paul McNeill
- Joni Mitchell
- Bobby Moore
- Mike Payne
- Alan Pepper
- Red Arrows
- Tom Rush
- Linda Thompson
- Richard Thompson
- Robin Williams

Dennis Wilson
Martin Windsor
Phillip Schofield
Prince Charles
Princess Diana
Mike Smith
Robin Smith
Redd Sullivan

Printed in Great Britain
by Amazon